H. RICHARD NIEBUHR

ABINGDON PILLARS
OF THEOLOGY

H. Richard Niebuhr

DONALD W. SHRIVER, JR.

Abingdon Press
Nashville

H. RICHARD NIEBUHR

This book is printed on acid-free paper.

Library of Congress Cataloging-in-Publication Data

Shriver, Donald W.
  H. Richard Niebuhr / Donald W. Shriver.
    p. cm.—(Abingdon pillars of theology)
  Includes bibliographical references and index.
  ISBN 978-0-687-65731-5 (pbk. : alk. paper)
  1. Niebuhr, H. Richard (Helmut Richard), 1894–1962. I. Title.
  BX4827.N47S57 2009
  230.092—dc22

2009004748

09 10 11 12 13 14 15 16 17 18—10 9 8 7 6 5 4 3 2 1

MANUFACTURED IN THE UNITED STATES OF AMERICA

CONTENTS

INTRODUCTION

Sometimes we feel in the midst of these many tasks in our vast world as though we were laborers in a giant factory where something is being made that we can never see. We are being required to stamp out this piece of sheet metal, to make this handle, to tighten this bolt—and to do all this over and over again without knowing what the whole process is all about. . . . But for the most part we fundamentally believe that something is going on, something is being accomplished. . . . We dimly see and hope that this is something glorious on which we are engaged. Something which, if we knew what it was, we could take pride in acknowledging as a work we had been allowed to serve.

In the summer of 2008, prefacing the worship service of a Presbyterian congregation in upper New York State, the above words appeared. They were excerpted from a sermon by H. Richard Niebuhr, "Man's Work and God's," based on Psalm 90.[1] There, a Hebrew poet celebrates the eternity of God and the finitude of all things human. One can read this psalm as a hymn of despair that humans and their works all vanish into nothing. But Niebuhr's take on the psalm was different. Some human deeds last a long time—witness, he said, this 2,500-year-old poem! But alas, in God's eternity two and a half millennia are not very long. None of us can be sure that anything we do or say will last forever. But faith in God affirms: there is Someone who is forever. Indeed, hope for the worth of our selves and our works appears at the end of the psalm: "Let the favor of the Lord our God be upon us; / And establish thou the work of our hands upon us" (verse 17 ASV).

Were he alive, I can imagine Niebuhr exclaiming to those forty congregants: "Thank you for deeming my words worth repeating. May they open a door for you to meet the God in whom the psalmist hoped!" Quite possibly, also, he might want to reply with both thanks and criticism to historian Martin Marty's 2008 nomination of him as one of the three greatest American theologians: "Jonathan Edwards, Reinhold Niebuhr, and H. Richard Niebuhr." He might have declined the nomination, though, more likely, he would simply have dismissed the project of contests between rival "greats."

Many readers of this page may find it surprising that two-thirds of Marty's greats came from one German-American family, and that the second born of these two brothers could really rank with the better-known firstborn. Certainly Reinhold Niebuhr belongs high on the eminence list of twentieth-century American theologians. Should this short book make the case for Marty's inclusion of the younger brother in his short list?

No. A book to prove the eminence deserved by H. Richard Niebuhr (HRN) would betray the spirit of the man about whom it is written. Once in the 1950s, he delivered a lecture at a leading East Coast seminary. Introducing him to the audience, the seminary president ended with the words, "And some of us think of him as an even greater theologian than his famous brother, Reinhold." Rising to speak, Niebuhr said sternly, "I thank the president for this introduction, but not for his final comparison of my brother and myself."

Such comparisons violated something deep in his intellectual commitments. In a long career as a teacher of Christian ethics at Yale Divinity School (1931–62), he encouraged students to understand theologians-past with due attention to the particular times and places in which they worked. How did they come to have faith in God? How did their time and place influence their work? What doubts did they struggle with? What expressions of loyalty to the all-encompassing will of God did they discern as mandated for themselves and their times? To dig deeply into these questions is to leave to God the judgment of who among one's predecessors is the greatest. If you study the past enough, you may find that divine honors belong to some surprising candidates. Look in history for "the least of these," the brothers and sisters of Jesus. Among them, arguments over who is the greatest are out of order. When it comes to greatness, God ought to dominate the field.

Yet not even God is a dominator after the image of human dictators. In Jesus, God came into human history in the form of a servant. Niebuhr always insisted that theology must pattern itself after that image. In an essay published in 1955, he defined his version of theological work in the context of university colleagues. Among academic disciplines,

> [It] can ask only for a place of service. It enters into the company of the sciences and studies not to be ministered to but to minister. . . . It does not presume to believe that because it is concerned with the knowledge of God it is preeminently his servant. . . . Its function is service to the church, by means of the criticism of actual religion and through the effort to help the church understand what it believes. The theology

which is servant to the church under God is also servant of the university and of political society, since it is not only the church that is in the kingdom of God and since faith exists and does its work not only in the church.[2]

Tolle lege. (Take up and read.) One can glimpse in the above excerpts from his writings that Niebuhr did not write about the ultimates of our knowledge of God in abstruse, esoteric, complex language. His are among the truly beautiful theological writings on any library shelf. To test this assertion I urge readers of this short text to take down a book or two by HRN from that shelf. In so urging, I follow the instruction given mysteriously to Augustine of Hippo. He tells in his *Confessions* how his conversion to Christian faith came to a critical moment when a child's song instructed him to pick up a letter of Paul and to read a certain verse in it (Romans 13:14). In doing so, Augustine walked through a door into personal acquaintance with the biblical testimony of Christians from three hundred years back. On the other side of that door, he found himself in the presence of the God and Father of Jesus Christ.

The writings of H. Richard Niebuhr are suffused with his attention to the possibility that, in every moment and circumstance, we humans are surrounded by the presence of One who is "above all that we ask or think." His books were not evangelistic tracts, nor did he expect all of his readers to be Christians. But he meant to move his readers to think, to struggle, to argue, and even to pray over the "existential" reality of a living faith in God. Theology for Niebuhr—as for his favorite American predecessor, Jonathan Edwards—is both a serious and a joyous exploration. From theological writing it is just possible that some readers will be led, in their own experience, to perceive and enjoy the glory of God.

That possibility cannot be tested at second- or thirdhand. This little book will fail in its purpose if any reader lets it substitute for consulting the writings of HRN himself. Indeed, he would have been the first to insist that his frequent allusions to the Bible were invitations to consult that text itself, which, in turn, must not become an idol that obscures the living presence of the One to whom those written words testify. The following pages will summarize most of Niebuhr's books, written over a period of thirty years. But to substitute a summary for the original can be a great mistake—as is the case with a college student who, asked by a teacher to read Shakespeare's *Romeo and Juliet*, skips the assignment saying, "Don't have to. I know the story already."

Someone has said that to listen to a symphony by Brahms is to hear a great mind at work. But you can't really get into Brahms by reading the concert program notes. This book is like program notes. It's a preface and invitation to the real thing.

A Life in the Twentieth Century

Allusions to his own biography are scarce in Niebuhr's writings, but they abound in sensitivity to world-historical change and the thinking of contemporary theologians and other thinkers. For a scholar who saw himself and all of us so deeply formed by our histories, it is important to trace some key points in the arc of his sixty-seven years.

Born September 3, 1894, in Wright City, Missouri, he was the youngest of the five children of Gustav and Lydia Niebuhr. She was the daughter of German immigrants, he an immigrant at age seventeen in 1878. As leaders of German-speaking congregations in the Midwest, both Gustav and his two pastor-sons became mediators of the classic Americanization of European immigrants. By the late nineteenth century they included more Germans than any other nationality.[3] Both brothers would be closely linked to the church of their father, the German Evangelical Synod of North America, and both would preside over transitions from German to English as first languages of their respective institutions.

Not until the 1920s would the younger Niebuhr regularly introduce himself as "Richard." In the family it was always "Helmut." At age fourteen he entered Elmhurst College, south of Chicago, whose one American-born professor, Samuel D. Press, would greatly influence his appropriation of the work of Adolf von Harnack and Reinhold Seeberg. He graduated from Elmhurst in 1912 and from Eden Seminary in 1915. In the meantime, in 1913, his father died at age fifty. In 1916 he followed in his father's footsteps by becoming a pastor of the Walnut Evangelical Church in St. Louis. Twenty years later, in a letter to his brother Reinhold, he would say, "I remain a preacher more than anything else."[4]

With the entry of the United States into the war with Germany in 1917, he volunteered as an Army chaplain, but the war ended before he was needed in France. Determined in 1919 to pursue graduate work in theology, he applied to Union Theological Seminary and Columbia University in New York. With the ink not yet dry on that application, his mentor, Press, now president of Eden Seminary, invited HRN to join its faculty. He set aside graduate plans and accepted the invitation. The next year he married Florence Marie Mittendorf, a member of the parish in Lincoln, Illinois, where his father had once been a pastor.

So far, one might say that HRN lived and worked in an immigrant cultural ghetto. But high German scholarship had opened him to the world of European theology. So after three years of teaching at Eden, he enrolled in Yale Divinity School in its BD and PhD programs.

His doctoral dissertation, *Ernst Troeltsch's Philosophy of Religion,* would become a basic plank in the structure of his future accounts of how religion, the church, and theological ideas always bear debts to nonreligious social influences. The book that would first make him famous—*The Social Sources of Denominationalism*—

grew out of his appreciation of Troeltsch. The Evangelical church was not about to forget the academic promise of an HRN, so in 1924 Elmhurst College invited him to become its president. Three years later Eden Seminary asked him to become its academic dean. His administrative sojourn at Elmhurst produced a critical change in its orientation from a German to a truly American institution. Niebuhr persuaded the faculty to teach in English, and, in other curricular ways, college ties with Germany shifted to America.

Experience as a college president, with all its conflicts over change, taxed his temperament, however, and at the end of three years he accepted a medically recommended respite. The Eden academic deanship suited him better, and four years in that position enabled him to complete *Social Sources* in 1929. The next year, joined by Reinhold, he spent eight months in Tubingen and Frankfort, ending with a trip to Moscow.

By now his scholarly reputation was rising, and in mid-1931 he had in hand an invitation to teach Christian Ethics on the faculty of Yale Divinity School. For the next thirty years, the drama of Richard Niebuhr's life transpired mostly in the interchanges between him, his students, his colleagues, and a growing number of intellectuals around the world. In those years his mind never went on "religious" retreat from the world. In his theological writings he would demand of himself an inexorable focus on the real, present, earthly experience of a faith that "conquers the world" (1 John 5:4) without deserting or despairing of the world. It would be thirty years pitted with the devastations of wars in Asia and Europe, on a scale unprecedented in history. In 1944 the horror of it all so depressed him that once again he sought medical treatment. How does a reasoning, feeling human being perceive God at work in the devastations of collective human sin, now so visible on a global scale? How can any human believe in God as one who is "powerful enough to engender confidence and good enough to merit loyalty" in a world like this?[5] He never let go of the questions, nor did they let go of him.

This book is a summary of a journey through the mind, heart, and work of a great American theologian. How he ranks with every other theologian is no matter of concern. How his attempt to commend faith in God and loyalty to "God's universal cause" matters a great deal indeed. May this road map encourage readers to join Niebuhr's journey in preparation for one of their own.

A Biographical
Chronology

Born in Wright City, Missouri, to Gustav and Lydia Niebuhr	September 3, 1894
Enrolled in Elmhurst College	1908
Graduated	1912
Enrolled in Eden Theological Seminary, St. Louis	1912
Death of his father	1913
Graduated from Eden	1915
Newspaper reporter, Lincoln, Illinois	1915–16
Ordained as minister in Walnut Park Evangelical Church, St. Louis	1916–17
Enlists as an Army chaplain at U.S. entry into the war	1917
Enrolls for graduate work at Union Theological Seminary, New York	Spring, 1919
Called instead to join the faculty of Eden Seminary	1919–22
Marries Florence Marie Mittendorf	June, 1920
Enrolls for BD and PhD degrees at Yale Divinity School	1922
Doctoral thesis, *Ernst Troeltsch's Philosophy of Religion*	1924
Called to presidency of Elmhurst College	1924–27
Called to Eden Seminary as academic dean	1927–31
The Social Sources of Denominationalism	1929
Sabbatical in Germany	1930–31
Called to faculty of Yale Divinity School	1931–62
Translates Paul Tillich's *The Religious Situation*	1932
Debates the ethics of war with Reinhold Niebuhr in *The Christian Century*	1932
The Kingdom of God in America	1937
The Meaning of Revelation	1941
Writings on the meaning of faith in a polytheistic culture	1942–60
Writes of war as "the judgment of God" and "crucifixion" in *The Christian Century*	1942–43
Christ and Culture	1951
The Purpose of the Church and Its Ministry	1956

FAITH AND IDOLATRY IN CHURCH HISTORY

The difficulty of the task of finding the via media *between adjustment to culture and compromise with prevailing social ethics cannot be an excuse for refusing to attempt it. The problem itself points to the need of some other type of Christianity than the religion which merely adjusts itself to social conditions whether these make for union or for schism. The church which seeks universality by means of such adjustment sacrifices its claims to universality. It becomes an organization intent upon the promotion of its own interests, without a sense of responsibility to the world as a social whole. And it loses its integrity in the very process of seeking universality, because its adjustments are made to a world which, far from being a universe, is divided in many ways. A universalism which is sought by adaptation only defeats itself.*[1]

In the year when HRN would be invited to Yale, Dietrich Bonhoeffer, German ecumenical fellow at Union Seminary in New York, wondered, with French fellow Jean Lassaire, what the future held for them both. What would each become? "I would like to be a saint," said Lassaire. "I would like to know how to have faith," countered Bonhoeffer.

Throughout his life as a theologian, Niebuhr never lost his own concern for the meaning, the origins, and the path of faith in God. Most of all, he kept focus on the distinction between "belief" in God and active response to the daily presence of God. Living in that presence was the test of real faith. Attentive as he was to the debts of every human present to the human past, he often insisted that really to worship the Lord of history as witnessed in the Bible is to acknowledge the presence of this Lord in every moment of time and at every juncture of space.

Theologies that insist on both the omnipresence and omnipotence of our Creator face the double challenge of discerning a humanly accessible location of the divine without turning that locus into a provincial idol. Niebuhr never ceased to struggle with this challenge. The term *postmodernism* was not yet prominent in his lifetime, but he knew very well how tempted humans are to settle down into some particular context of time, space, experience, knowledge, and belief, and thus to become happily "provincial." To adjust to the booming, buzzing confusion of life, perhaps one needs only Voltaire's rule: cultivate your own garden. That rule will often work in one's pursuit of happiness. But it does not always work. When some outside power invades our private time and space, do we yield to it? When the nation calls us to serve it in a war? When one has to choose between two job offers? When the love goes out of a marriage, leaving behind doubt that no human love is to be trusted? When the politicians we voted for betray the causes we thought they stood for?

From first to last in his writings, Niebuhr asked himself and others: is there any object of trust and loyalty that will never betray us? Even to ask the question can be on the verge of faith in the God of Abraham, the Father of Jesus. It is also to ask about the possibility of human access to the ultimately trustworthy object who is God, "high and lifted up" (Isaiah 6:1 KJV) but also "on earth as it is in heaven" (Matthew 6:10), and "very near to you . . . in your mouth and in your heart" (Deuteronomy 30:14). Whatever else it may mean to have faith in *any* god, it has to mean adherence to an ultimate Authority to whom all other authorities are and ought to be related.

Relationships that make a human life human were always central for HRN's empirical and normative descriptions of who we are and what we might become. One of our crucial life-works has to be the discovery of persons, organizations, principles, and hopes worthy of unflagging trust and loyalty. Experience may convince us that no relation is that worthy, but in fact we can hardly survive without trusting someone or something by which we can discern and live with the fallibility of all other objects of trust. The dilemma is real: threatened trust, necessary trust.

Understanding faith as a compound of ultimate trust and ultimate loyalty preoccupied HRN lifelong. He prized Martin Luther's classic definition, "Whatever thy heart clings to and relies upon, that is properly thy God."

> When we believe that life is worth living by the same act we refer to some being which makes our life worth living. We never merely believe that life is worth living, but always think of it as made worth living by something on which we rely.[2]

In fact, over time, most of us rely on many things, persons, causes, institutions, and ideas. The jumble of it all may never worry us until one and another of these objects prove unreliable, so that we prudently narrow down our range of deep trust. Even then, we are unlikely to let go of multiple loves, hopes, and reliances. We then can honestly confess that we are natural polytheists. In light of multiple human needs and desires, people and cultures multiply their gods. Pragmatically, one never knows when another member of the pantheon may have to be appealed to.

Is there, then, a single ultimately reliable object of faith? Spiritual descendants of Abraham and Jesus answer yes. How others can make the same answer is central in most of HRN's writings but especially central to his third book, *The Meaning of Revelation.* To that book we will turn our attention in chapter 3. For the moment, it is important to note that, for all his respect for our inbred ability to reason our way through the forest of candidates for trust, the descendants of Abraham and Jesus confess that they have not discovered the Ultimate but rather have been discovered by it. We have been given God in God's self-revelation "in our human history." We have received "a great gift. We say that it is given, that it has been given, that it is being given, and that when it is received very profound consequences follow."[3]

Church History as the Long Wrestle with Idolatry

Social Sources

One large consequence in the history of the Christian churches has been the perennial struggle of its leaders and members to respect the "treasure in earthen vessels," which is the self-revelation of God in Abraham and Sarah, all the prophets of Israel, the unique faithfulness of Jesus Christ, and the continued faithful presence of the Holy Spirit to the church and to the world. "Earthen vessel," in the famous Pauline image (2 Corinthians 4:7 RSV), calls for distinctions between the container and the thing contained, "to show that the transcendent power belongs to God and not to us." In a nutshell, the travail of church history is the saga of remembering, forgetting, and re-remembering this distinction.

Social Sources is the most sociological of HRN's books, but all of its careful readers know that it is sociology and history fused with consistent theological criticism. The blend of empirical history and normative is intimate here. The era of the late 1920s in which he wrote had been preceded by large efforts among world church leaders to reknit the tattered fabric of separated segments of the Christian movement, a concern that comported with Niebuhr's own concern for a faith worth calling "universal," that is, related to the whole of Creation and the whole of history. A deeply divided church was a poor missionary to the divided world of human society. The one's divisions were shaped by the other's, yielding the infidelity of a church that confused reasons of faith with reasons of sinful provincialism as it blithely justified another sundering of the body of Christ.

The influence of Ernst Troeltsch pervades this study; but, as later work would make clearer, HRN does not strip all value from the ordinary influences of personal experience, social condition, and reigning ideology on the beliefs and actions of churches. "Earthen vessels" have value, especially when soundly related to their treasures. But right relation to such treasure means maintaining the status of the

3

container as part of a divine creation that must never be accorded the worship due only to the Creator. To let the two merge into one is idolatry.

Many are the occasions in which, over two millennia, Christians and their institutions have fallen into idolatry. Niebuhr classifies the sources of idolatry in this history along the spectrum of social classes, political powers, sectional rivalries, racism, and social mobility. Like Troeltsch and Max Weber, he surveys this history with acute appreciation of the mixture of all theologies with the distorting compromises of adjustments to changing human circumstance. For example,

> the Luther who began the Reformation belonged to mankind.[4]. . . But the Luther who founded the Lutheran church as a separate, nationalist denomination was a Germanized Luther, who needed to attenuate his heroic conceptions in order that German nationalism might save Christianity from its Latinic degeneracy. . . . In the end [many of the other Reformation] churches became nations at prayer, but even in prayer Christians found it difficult to transcend the limitations of national consciousness.[5]

The Churches of the Disinherited

A generation before the rise of Liberation Theology, Niebuhr read the prophets of Israel, the teachings of Jesus, and the practice of the early church as setting an ethical priority on the needs of the poor, who share with the rich equal dignity in the eyes of God. Economic forces in society he saw as the major source of frequent contradiction to this ethic in the actual shifts of internal culture and organization of the churches. We know that the contradiction was already appearing in Pauline church life (1 Corinthians 1:26-31, 11:17-22). HRN sees it displayed across 2,000 years of church history. "It began as a religion of the poor, of those who had been denied a stake in contemporary civilization," but it became a church that echoed the class divisions of its surrounding society.[6]

Thus began the historic social dynamic recorded by Troeltsch and Weber: the neglected poor form their own church, they become richer, in turn they neglect a new generation of poor, and finally the latter tend either to accept their subordination to their "betters" or they split and form another church. "This pattern recurs with remarkable regularity in the history of Christianity."[7] Medieval Catholicism adjusted to the phenomenon by permitting monks to identify with the poor while the "secular" church hierarchy accumulated great wealth. With the Protestant Reformation the new middle classes found a home in Lutheran and Calvinist state churches, but not often did the poor feel at home there either. Instead, some revolted and formed their own sects, which often were ruthlessly put down by governments encouraged by reformed churches. The proclaimed ethics of the latter often focused on "freeing men from the sins of luxury and sensuality rather than from the evils of injustice and inequality" in society.[8] This Protestant stress on individualism in ethics would persist well into future centuries and especially in America. Meantime, in the internal life of their congregations, sectarians often isolated themselves from their neighbors, poor and rich, so that they too risked becoming exclusive castes. Thus, said Niebuhr, comes "the tragedy of caste in the church of Christ, for castes make outcasts and outcasts form castes."[9]

Niebuhr's attention to the Methodist movement of the eighteenth and nineteenth centuries is especially thorough and relevant to American church history. He calls Methodism "the last great religious revolution of the disinherited in Christendom."[10] As stressed by John Wesley, ethics for Methodists largely concerned personal behavior. It was hospitable to middle-class aspirations. Though other scholars would advance the theory that English Methodism, in its organization of small "classes" in its chapels, trained its converts in the arts of group leadership and so laid the groundwork for the coming of the English Labor Party, the work of conceptualizing the injustices of classism and call for real social revolution was left to the nineteenth-century labors of one Karl Marx.

The conclusion of this and ensuing surveys of church history in *Social Sources* moves toward the sober conclusion that every religious structure in this history exhibits imperfection in light of standards proper to its own traditions. Indeed, judged by the faith and ethics of the New Testament, the proclaimed standards themselves are defective as well as members' conformity to them. Niebuhr's contemporary Paul Tillich said that real Protestantism has to be perpetually dissatisfied with its own achievements. He called this "the Protestant principle." Every reformation must eventually be reformed. The ethical corollary of this principle, HRN would insist by the end of the book, was God's requirement of humans that we perennially open ourselves to *repentance*, what he would later call "perpetual revolution."

The Churches of the Middle Class

Middle-class churches are especially important for American church history, and Niebuhr's focus in his second book of 1937 will look at those churches from another angle—not how the society shaped the churches, but how the churches sometimes shaped the society. Neither he nor his European mentors Troeltsch and Weber saw religious organizations as wholly determined by social-economic forces, as Marxism was prone to do. *Social Sources* focuses on those forces. HRN wants to demonstrate that differences of doctrine do not alone account for the differences of various Christian groups in history.

He lists the interests that seem natural to the new middle class—people who are breaking with old economic traditions and taking initiatives to create wealth for themselves: love of personal rights and liberty; an activist attitude toward daily life; trust in personal effort, not fate, as the determiner of one's earthly destiny. Such dispositions affect the churches of the middle class early and late in Protestantism. They shape doctrines of God's ceaseless activity and the Christian life as active. Sin now consists of deeds rather than corruptions of nature. Righteousness is first of all obedience to the will of God, and "salvation is conceived as a process within the individual, not the construction of a divine kingdom."[11] The economic ethic associated with these doctrines stresses "honesty, industry, sobriety, thrift, and prudence," and how poverty arises from moral failure. Protestants found some balance to this individualism in their concern for family morals, but for the most part "this morality is incapable of developing a hopeful passion for social justice. Its martyrs die for liberty not for fraternity and equality."[12]

Niebuhr's recounting of these Protestant tendencies is complex and historically "thick." He makes clear, for example, that the stern economic disciplines mandated by John Calvin in Geneva deteriorated in the next generation under the pressures of the business interests of the commercial class. Gone was Calvin's suspicion of "usury" and the temptations of wealth; gone too the obligation of the church to exercise collective judgment of the behavior of its members. Instead, individual conscience became ultimate law and with it "the self-sufficiency of economic ethics" divorced from the warnings against idolatries of wealth in the teachings of Jesus.[13]

Readers of this and other chapters of *Social Sources* may find themselves quarreling with one or another of his critical studies of their own respective church traditions. Methodists, for example, may find themselves quarreling with his view that Methodism had a very weak social ethic, just as Presbyterians may protest that their form of church government is not really "autocratic."[14] No doubt Niebuhr means to bring all of his readers eventually to an experience of uncomfortable criticism of many of their favorite, previously unexamined preferences. It is worth noting that, in criticizing the "bourgeois churches," he is reflecting on his own upbringing in a Lutheran congregation in St. Louis.

Nationalism and the Churches

Born in the shadow and without the permission of the Roman Empire, the Christian movement struggled to survive against imperial power for almost three centuries. Occasionally, the Apostle Paul shrewdly exploited his Roman citizenship, however, for preserving his freedom to preach the gospel. With the coming of the Age of Constantine, Christians breathed sighs of relief that at last government was its protector. More: within some seventy-five years, sensing that the empire needed propping up by the new faith, Rome decreed that Christianity was to be the only *religio licita*. Soon after that, the empire crumbled under assault from "barbarian" invasions, and now Christians trembled at the prospect that the government, now their friend, no longer had the power to protect them.

Against that fear Augustine wrote *The City of God*, assuring Christians that they belonged to a city more eternal than Rome, a kingdom of God that no earthly power could shake. Nonetheless, yearning for comfortable, protective relation to political powers persisted into the rest of church history. Numerous groups of churches, in all of this history, took names and ecclesiastical identity from their origins in particular national settings. Niebuhr documents this phenomenon in a two-page listing of some fifty contemporary church bodies, so self-identified, in the United States alone. Ours, he writes, is a "pot-pourri of churches," each proudly separated from the others by a memory of national roots in history and national culture that shape theology, liturgy, and ethical practice.[15]

Earnest theological debates, which produced some of the dominant theological creeds, for example, depended in their very origin on overt connections of church and state. From the Nicene Creed of 325 C.E. to the Westminster confession of 1647, governments hosted the learned debates and put their stamp of legitimacy on the creeds. Niebuhr exempts no large church tradition from this critique: the Catholic church that still identifies itself as Roman, the Eastern Orthodox churches who in name and polity are nationally separate from each other, the Protestant churches who began in revolt against state churches—one and all bear the marks of some earthly city provincially distinct from the universal fellowship of Christians to whose heavenly destiny Augustine witnessed. "The acceptance of national culture goes hand in hand with the acceptance of national sovereignty as divinely ordained and of established social customs as divinely sanctioned."[16] The American cases of these tendencies have their own differences from the European. HRN will give much attention to the former in his next book; but it will be evident to any student of American church life in 2009 that intimate connections between being Christian and being American pervade the minds of numerous Christians across the spectrum from Catholic to Protestant to sectarian in this country.

Is Christian identity profoundly tied to national identity? Or is such a tie idolatrous and a compromise to a humanity-focused faith? For the rest of his life, HRN would insist on the importance of the question and the difficulty many Christians have in being sure of the answer.

Sectionalism and Denominationalism in America

In the final chapters of *Social Sources* Niebuhr focuses on America. His three remaining areas of analysis cross-cut each other sociologically and historically: We are a nation so large geographically that we often think of each other according to the section of the country where we live; we are a nation of immigrants, who bring their own former national loyalties with them; and we are a country whose history has been tragically shaped around the legacies of slavery and racism.

So many are the "sections" of American history that Niebuhr devotes more pages (65) to this theme than to any other in the book. The sections are both geographical and social: North-South, urban-rural; settled East-frontier West, industrial-agricultural, local-state-federal rivalries for power. The great sectional conflict that led to the Civil War prompts his acerbic observation that, having split internally over questions of slavery and state versus federal loyalties, several large denominations (Methodist, Baptist, Presbyterian) maintained their sectional identities long into the postwar future.[17] Particularly influential, he observes, following Frederick Jackson Turner, was the "frontier mentality," with its emphasis on individual initiative, mobility, anti-mercantilism, and small community life. Fueling antagonism between the mind of the Easterner against the mind and habits of the frontier were opinions like that of Timothy Dwight, New England Congregationalist. The frontiersman, he said, is "too idle; too talkative; too passionate; too prodigal; and too shiftless to acquire either property or character."[18] In church records of New York State HRN discovers one body's stated opinion of Rhode Island as "the receptacle of all sorts of riff-raff people" making that tiny region "nothing else than the sewer (*latrina*) of New England."[19]

In contrast, the missionary commitments of most of the eastern denominational leaders impelled them to insist that frontier people were beloved of God too. That insistence sent Baptist and Methodist missionaries to the frontiers for preaching the gospel and for setting up new congregations whose internal culture and theology came to reflect many frontier values. Alongside these established denominations was the fervor of the sectarians, who, in the Second Great Awakening, "by contagion in the excitable atmosphere of nineteenth-century America, infected the whole nation with the spirit of utopianism, religious impressionism, and emotional mobility."[20]

HRN brings his analysis of sectionalism to bear on the famous political and religious work of William Jennings Bryan.

> In recent times the conflict between urban and rural religion took on dramatic form in the theological battles of Modernism and Fundamentalism. The agrarian leader of the West, Bryan, became not only the champion of its economic interests but of its religion also. In the religious position he and his followers represented were reflected not only the memories and habits of frontier faith but also the experiences of rural life. Modernism, however, grew out of the social experience of the city bourgeoisie as well as out of the impact of the new science on religion.[21]

Niebuhr sees the religious experience of the plains and the isolated farm as a setting that encourages converts to center on personal relation to the grace of God, "while urban religion is more concerned with the gain of that same grace that men may live at peace with one another" in the crowded, pluralistic city.[22]

The most notorious influence of sectionalism on economics, politics, and religious social views in America circled around the tortured issue of slavery. HRN takes up this issue again in his next-to-last chapter on "The Color Line." Here, at the conclusion of his empathic accounts of how division over slavery led to internal and external division of churches, he observes sadly how, in this history, "there arose the passions of conflict which accompany the strife of those who cannot understand the apparent moral obtuseness of their enemy."[23] In future writings HRN will frequently return to this affront to a hope for a universal human community envisioned in the New Testament. Humans are prone to disdain and murder each other for a dense mixture of interests economic, political, ideological, and religious. For this all-pervasive circumstance, there is no remedy but repentance.

The Churches of the Immigrants

A large swathe of American church history follows wave after wave of European national-ethnic groups who, leaving the settled churches of an Old World had to reconstruct some solidarity for themselves in the New. "The only organization which was readily at hand for maintaining the unity of the group was the church."[24] In this chapter HRN writes with detailed knowledge of the ambivalences that beset his own immigrant heritage of German Lutheranism. Like other groups, its leaders confronted a double challenge: to adjust to a new society with its new prolixity of other churches and to maintain their own integrity in organization, theology, and liturgy. Early on, adjustment and imitation of earlier arrivals often dominated, but later on imitation gave way to withdrawal into defensive orthodoxies. The latter often owed more to the cultural legacies of the old country than to distinctive Christian beliefs and ethics. In this process, ecumenical peace vied with increasing internal and external sectarian splits, fueled not only by diversities of cultural roots but also by the resentments of the "natives" (i.e., second and third generations of earlier immigrants) toward the newcomers. These conflicts yielded a uniquely intense American set of religious-social controversies. HRN describes these conflicts with subtle attention to detail, and it is clear that the tension between ecumenical and particularistic dynamics in American church history will be an issue that his faith and ethics will not permit him to set aside in his future work.

Denominationalism and the Color Line

If there is one issue in *Social Sources* that arouses his theological-ethical passion, however, it is the awful history of slavery and racism and their deep corruptions of church life in America. Niebuhr sees racism in American churches as a unique case of the triumph of an anthropological theory over theological roots. "After the close association of Jews and Gentiles in early Christianity had ceased, the question of race relations in the church of Christ did not emerge again as a challenging problem until modern times."[25] Racism of some sort may in fact root in many earlier strands of Western culture, but HRN's horror at the American case centers on the ease with which the churches accepted the inferiority of black "immigrants" without theological qualm. A number of the "founding fathers" of the new nation had guilty consciences over the conflict between the ideals of their

Declaration of Independence and the presence of black slaves in the land, but as the eighteenth became the nineteenth century, numerous church leaders turned blind eyes to the scandalous contradictions of slavery to both democracy and the New Testament. Yielding to economic and political interests, some theologians even draped the scandal in clothes of theological legitimacy.

As a whole, however, the churches were not so completely blind to the humanity of black slaves as to deny that they should have the gospel preached to them. Some Christian slaveholders might deny even that duty; but adjustment to their economic interests came forth from some theologians in their insistence that the "bodies" and the "souls" of slaves were different: the one might remain in outward servitude while the other was blessed by the grace of God. The result, which HRN records in demographic detail, was a growing presence of black members in antebellum Protestant churches, albeit in inferior status. In postwar times they mostly withdrew into their own congregations and denominations. HRN regards this divorce from "association without equality" as a justified step toward "the ultimately desirable fellowship of equals" promised Christians in the New Testament church. But the very existence in his century of segregated denominations Niebuhr regards as a standing rebuke to earlier failures of churches to resist the lures of profitable racism.

The pain that haunts this chapter of *Social Sources* is palpable. A church comfortable in its racism has for HRN "sometimes the sad sound of irony, and sometimes falls upon the ear as unconscious hypocrisy—but sometimes there is in it the bitter cry of repentance."[26]

By What Measures, Repentance?

It is clear from the first chapter of this book that Niebuhr sees denominations as more a betrayal than a reflection of original Christian revelation. Indeed, these historically rich chapters in church history may leave the impression among readers that there is little to celebrate theologically in it at all. As we shall see, *The Kingdom of God in America* seeks to redress this impression. An additional criticism of *Social Sources* might be that the ethical standards by which church infidelity is to be judged appear only implicitly from time to time in these pages.

The last chapter, "Ways to Unity," is something of a redress, however, as it confessionally lays out Niebuhr's hopes for Christian churches repentant of their schismatic, provincialist, classist, racist sins. Here he identifies the positive theo-ethic yardsticks for measuring the integrities and the corruptions of church history.

- The primacy in biblical ethics of justice for the poor.
- The requirement of love and unity-in-diversity in the church.
- Need, not status, as the rule for distribution of economic resources in the church between the rich and the poor, in the church and in the society.

- The principle of nonviolence and forgiveness toward enemies.
- The inadmissibility of all versions of caste to church life and practice.
- The transcendence of loyalty to the God and Father of Jesus Christ over all cultural and church loyalty, which means perpetual struggle in the church to perceive the distinctions.

By the same token, here and there in *Social Sources*, HRN admires occasions in this history when some body of Christians has matched their behavior to such standards: the honesty of identification with the poor of society among the sects and monastics; the resistance of some churches—for example, American Episcopalians in the face of the Civil War—to the temptation of schism; the real if ambiguous welcome that antebellum congregations offered to converted slaves; the less ambiguous postwar decision of the latter to seek equality in their own congregations; and the insistence of Reformation leaders, at their best, that every reformation needs its continuing repentant re-forming. Significant too in this last chapter is Niebuhr's reversal of emphasis for which his brother was to become identified in his soon-to-be-published *Moral Man and Immoral Society* (1932). Not necessarily so: individuals can be more corrupt than institutions. The latter are sometimes better guides to ethical behavior than are the flawed consciences of their members.[27] HRN believed that reformation emerges less from the formal institutional structures of churches than from the movements initiated by leaders like St. Francis and George Fox. Such "movements of the spirit" have "penetrated" the evil structures of slavery, war, economic injustice, and classism with a "fellowship of love" endemic to the real followers of Jesus. "The increase of that fellowship today is the hope of Christendom and of the world."[28]

The language of this concluding chapter of the book will be familiar to many students of the theological era in which HRN was raised. It is language, as Gary Dorrien might say, "straight out of the liberal playbook,"[29] with its emphasis on personal consciousness of God, the role of Kant's practical reason for carrying out in the world the ethics of the gospel, the necessity of choices between the better and the worse elements of human cultures, the church as a community movement rather than an institution defined by doctrines, and "divine love upon which all stable and just social life must be built." In many writings to come, HRN would express strong criticism of liberal Protestantism of his time. But he leveled like criticism at a movement associated with his contemporary Karl Barth, whose critique of "culture Protestantism" Niebuhr admired. But the Barthian rejection of everything "religious" as human arrogance before God, he rejected. Not everything in either secular culture or organized religion, said he, is antagonistic to the ethics of the Bible. Further, in a church and secular world many an ethical decision requires, not obedience to absolute good and resistance to absolute evil, but choices between gray mixtures of black and white. Neither surrender to the world nor escape from the world is an option for the ethical reflection and action of the faithful church. Instead,

11

> Is there not available some form of the Christian faith which possesses both the compelling ideal that can bring inner unity to the world and courage to undertake the penetration of human society with that ideal despite the difficulties and confusions which tempt to surrender or to flight?[30]

This too is the language of theological liberalism. It forecasts an agenda for Niebuhr's future work on the tension between a transcendent loyalty to God and the mundane tasks of faithful Christians.

The last page of *Social Sources* is an eloquent summary of the theme that has dominated the book: a biblically measured faith and ethic require Christians to confess their sins of caste and other rejections of divine inclusiveness and to repent. "The road to unity is the road of repentance. . . . It requires that Christians learn to look upon their separate establishments and exclusive creeds with contrition rather than pride." Once setting their feet on that road, Christians will be in touch with "a Kingdom of God that is among us."[31]

How that Kingdom, in glints and flashes, has been among us in a place called America became the theme, eight years later, of HRN's next book.

Questions for Reflection

1. Because *Social Sources* specializes in negative indictments of churches for their failure to live up to the ethical precedents of the New Testament, might the book be likely to persuade some readers that, after all, "organized religion" is a lost cause?

2. Is the human self more to be trusted than a church to be "untarnished by the world" (James 1:27 NEB)? When it comes to repentance, might Reinhold Niebuhr be right in thinking that personal repentance is easier to achieve than repentance by a group?

3. Max Weber observed that religious bodies seldom are the sole causes of major change in a society. But religion sometimes supplies "switching points" in movement toward social change. Some would say that the Civil Rights Movement, which began in Niebuhr's latter years, was such a point in American history. Is this a credible claim? What other historical illustrations?

4. "Between the white and the black of absolute good and absolute evil there are infinite numbers of shades of gray and between any two of these shades there may be vast and important distinctions."[32] What does this belief have to say about faith, ethics, and compromises that may be necessary and desirable in the living of a Christian life? So far, do you detect in Niebuhr's writings helpful ethical guidance to churches for navigating between "light gray" and "dark gray" compromises?

CHAPTER TWO

THE KINGDOM OF GOD IN AMERICA

Every movement, like every person, needs to be understood before it can be criticized. And no movement can be understood until its presuppositions, the fundamental faith upon which it rests, have been at least provisionally adopted. The presuppositions may not be our own; we may find good reason for rejecting them in favor of others; but we cannot understand without occupying a standpoint, and there is no greater barrier to understanding than the assumption that the standpoint which we happen to occupy is a universal one, while that of the object of our criticism is relative.[1]

Some years ago I heard an academic colleague quoted as having said, unkindly, of another, "He wrote only one book, but he wrote it ten times." That remark could never come from careful readers of HRN's half dozen major works. He corrected himself from book to book, and each one was likely to be counted a landmark in the typography of American theology. In this bent toward self-correction, he practiced what he preached: perpetual intellectual re-formation.

As a seminary teacher at Eden and then (from 1931) at Yale Divinity School, he faced classes of ministerial students who would soon be required to help congregations understand not only "the social sources" of their history-shaped faith but also the possible enduring truth in it. Writing in the preface of his 1937 book, he conceded that sociological critiques of the history of Christianity "could deal with the religion which was dependent on culture [but] it left unexplained the faith which is independent, which is aggressive rather than passive, and which molds culture instead of being molded by it."[2] Troeltsch and Weber might illuminate the nonreligious influences upon religion, but their work—like *Social Sources*—could leave the impression that the authentic, unifying, persisting claims of Christian faith were always under an obscuring cloud in the history of the church. Not so, Niebuhr had noted on some pages of his 1929 book; but in *The*

Kingdom of God in America he reverses the emphasis, turning to a review of American church history under the theme: in what times and ways have the churches exhibited positive influence on their culture and authentic continuity with their biblical origins?

Faith, history, and theological thinking were in perpetual conversation in Niebuhr's academic work. His concepts of human selfhood, social institutions, and cultural ideas he understood as forever and inherently social and historical. In his preface to *Kingdom*, he identified himself as "one who feels the need of testing the abstract ideas of theology and ethics in the laboratory of history."[3] Deep in this method was his belief that the ideas and the experience of Christians through the ages are *dialectic* in form, that is, two-sided, interactive, history shaped and history shaping. The current book, he conceded, "may seem to be an effort to present theology in the guise of history, yet the theology has grown out of the history as much as the history has grown out of the theology."[4] He goes on to note that, in his own careful study of the materials that open our windows to the past, he has tried not to "squeeze" the historical facts into a theological mold, nor to ignore the ways in which theologies have themselves molded the history. This dialectic, he frequently insisted, must not be confused with dualism, paradox, or mere contradiction. A dialectic embodies two sides of one reality. It pays tribute to the multiplicity of reality as humans perceive it, but it also is a way of doing justice to the search for unity in the multiplicity. Above all, HRN seeks to identify instances of Christian faithfulness in a history that records many an infidelity.

Out of fidelity to the materials, he concluded that three centuries of American church history—seventeenth, eighteenth, and nineteenth—could be broadly described under dominant themes, each of which embraced continuity with the roots of Christianity while reflecting a response to the particularities of changing American culture. With many professional historians, he knew that history cannot be understood or summarized without the aid of typology—that is, images of a range of complex facts which, like mountains, are best comprehended with the guidance of a survey-based silhouette of the whole.

From his own surveys, HRN found three theological variations on the classic Christian, especially Protestant, theology in the witness of American churches in the three centuries: the Sovereignty of God, the Reign of Christ, and the Kingdom on Earth. Whether these summary images have validity, he would be the first to say, can only be tested against the details of the history. Many pages of *The Kingdom of God in America* are rich in those details.

The Sovereignty of God: The Seventeenth Century

Before tending to the substance of these three themes, he writes a second introductory chapter, "The Problem of Constructive Protestantism," in which he probes the distinctive understanding of the sovereignty of God in the theology of the Protestant founders. Anyone seeking an astute, balanced summary of the essential Protestant version of Christian faith will find nothing better in recent theological literature than this chapter. The tensions in Protestant thought, Niebuhr observes, grow out of the Protestant Principle. Here is his careful statement of that problem:

> The dilemma of Protestantism lay . . . in these factors: it had no will to power and in view of its positive principle could have none, for supreme power belonged only to God and evil resulted from every human arrogation of his dominion; it had no definite idea of the end toward which it was traveling and could have none, since the future lay with the free God; and it could not be ruthless since it had the inhibiting commandments of the gospel ever before it. As a theory of *divine* construction the Protestant movement was hard put to it to provide principles for human construction. Yet it was unable to be supine, awaiting in patience what God might do, since it was evident that men lived in crisis and that they could not stand still but were hastening either to destruction or to life. It was necessary to press into the kingdom.[5]

In a time when the idea of "sovereignty" seems mismatched to much talk in the American life of freedom, HRN's phrase "the free God" echoes Karl Barth's favorite word for the divine sovereignty.[6] The important note in this subtle description of the Protestant spirit is its insistence on the obligation of the faithful to enact concrete expressions of their obedience to God in the expectation that this very obedience will be subject to reformation—in a future generation if not in one's own.

For the hundred years during and after the lives of its founders, Protestantism in Europe accentuated protest against its medieval predecessors in theology and church-state relations. This struggle came to a tortured climax in the Thirty Years' War (1618–48) and resulted in the compromises of the Treaty of Westphalia, which permitted local monarchs to choose whether the religion of their respective territories would be Catholic or Protestant. Thus, in these very decades, against the mixed blessing of this compromising peace, "America became the land of opportunity. Here Protestantism could turn from protest and conflict to construction" of its own church life and its own secular government.[7] And here, in a land sparsely populated and rich in resources of land, its leaders could work out their theology and ethic of the Sovereign Lord with due attention to the dialectics of the Protestant problem.

In their seventeenth-century "errand into the wilderness," America Protestant leaders seldom framed their project along lines of Thomas More's "utopia" or any perfectionist ideal for a new society. Always in their rhetoric Pilgrims and Puritans spoke of their new colonies as relative, partial steps toward a kingdom whose perfection lay in God's future, not in present human constructions. In this project, *contra* their popular reputation, neither the Calvinists of Geneva nor their disciples of Massachusetts were "theocrats." God's unmediated rule of the world permits no direct translation into any human idea or social arrangement. A theocracy the universe is, but no government or church is its trustworthy embodiment. Forgetting this, Protestantism forgets itself. New institutions, yes, but never as full remedy for human fallibility; human reason and human will, but no promise of perfection from them. Sobriety and realism were hallmarks of this attitude and lifestyle.

> They were for the most part thoroughly convinced that mankind had somehow been corrupted; they knew that the order of glory had not yet been established; they were pilgrims all who did not expect to be satisfied in the time of their pilgrimage.[8]

Meantime, however, they put together colonies with concrete expressions of their faith in the sovereignty of God: a tentative social structure, which Niebuhr calls a constitution. In it there were separate church and secular governments, each with curbs on every tendency of human beings to ignore their finitude. Niebuhr is ambiguous in his description of the Puritan "constitution" as less a set of laws as a commitment to move forever in a Protestant "zigzag" between the wisdom of Scripture and the inner light of the Spirit.[9] Like their peers in revolutionary England in the 1640s, for them every structure was subject to reform. Government-by-discussion would become a principled substitute for government-by-kingly-decree, and this principle would be basic to the newly constituted state. But Puritan-dominated government could be wrong too; and for identifying that wrong the Sovereign Ruler of the world uses a church independent of worldly government. They had to be "a church before they were a commonwealth."[10] Organizing the church, in fact, was for them their first duty; how else could any society be supplied with a steady witness to the kingship of the Almighty? That witness, of course, comes to bear on the church itself, whose gathered community must frequently ask itself: of what sins does God now require us too to repent?

Niebuhr dwells at length in the conclusion of his chapter on seventeenth-century Protestant leaders' influence, not often credited to them, on the political spirit and substance of the Constitution-makers of Philadelphia in 1787. He quotes James Bryce's famous word, "It is the work of men who believed in original sin." Their insistence on limited government was an outgrowth of the certainty that ultimate power belongs to God and to no human agency whatsoever. That certainty required a church free from the coercions of government and a government free of arrogance and respectful of power limits. Having established these limits, both government and church could undertake their proper services to public need, an undertaking that began to flourish in new ways in the period that Niebuhr names "The Kingdom of Christ."

The Kingdom of Christ: The Eighteenth and Nineteenth Centuries

By discerning three emerging theo-ethical profiles in three respective centuries of American Protestant life, HRN does not mean to separate certain peaks of the history from the rest of the range. God rules the world, rules it in the grace of Jesus Christ in the hearts and lives of the faithful, and will rule it in a kingdom coming in the future. None of these themes lacks connection to the others. But as the centuries passed, one and another peaked in the preaching, the worship, and the ministry of developing Protestant churches.

Among the limits that the divine sovereignty mandated for humans was that, as God was free to attend to the created world, so the free individual was free to attend to the needs of the neighbor. Echoing Luther, this was ethical disciplining of sheer individualism. Good works for the good of the neighbor were not an add-on but a necessary outgrowth of the human self converted to the rule of God and, more specifically, the liberating power of the spirit of Jesus Christ.

Rightly to be subject to this rule required a transformation of inner spirit and outer behavior, which eighteenth-century Protestant preachers came to call an "awakening," repentance from old self-centered ways of life and a birth of love for every one of God's creatures. The American prophet of this awakening in the mid-eighteenth century was Jonathan Edwards. The Hebrew prophet who presaged these inner-outer transformations of human being was Jeremiah. Niebuhr quotes Jeremiah 31:31-34 with its promise of God's New Covenant with humans, a new law "in their inward parts" (v. 33 KJV), forgiveness of their sins, and free spontaneous obedience to the will of God springing from inwardly transformed hearts.

Niebuhr found the Quakers of the eighteenth century authentic embodiments of the new accent on inward-outward spiritual change.

> They were more interested in the kingdom of Christ than in the sovereignty of God; that is to say, they were impressed even more by the fact that the kingdom had come and could come to men in their own lives, bringing liberty and joy, than by the fact that universal law and justice reigned throughout the spheres.

It is a side of the Puritan heritage not often remembered in contemporary popular American opinion.

> The kingdom of God is not a reign of terror but one of love, not of law but of liberty. God has willed to reconcile men to his will, to write his law upon their hearts, and he has done this by means of Jesus Christ. . . . [The converted person] is no longer concerned about himself and can love goodness for its own sake.[11]

There follow a dozen pages of description of the spiritual-ethical accents of the gospel preaching of the revivalists, Jonathan Edwards in particular. These passages are an eloquent introduction to the new, psychologically oriented theology of Edwards, who, in appropriating some of the new sciences of the European Enlightenment, invited his educated congregation to experience the transforming power of the Holy Spirit. Edwards was intent on linking faith in the divine sovereignty to the discernable acts of the Sovereign among living men and women. New ideals, mere objective knowledge, and new efforts of will power were insufficient for transforming persons and their relations to one another. Niebuhr is eloquent in his appropriation of the spirit of Edwards when he writes:

> The kingdom of God was the rule of sincerity in lives which had been made to understand the deviousness and trickery of the well loved ego as it skulks and hides in the labyrinthine ways of the mind, and which, having been made to see that they lived by forgiveness and not merit, indeed no longer needed to defend themselves against themselves, their fellow men and God.[12]

European rationalism, called Enlightenment, bore down on minds and consciences of literate Americans in this era. Philosophers like John Locke insisted that the human mind begins to perceive truth about the world through sense impressions; but theologians of the Awakenings were diligent to distinguish that truth from "saving truth." One Presbyterian, like Edwards, wrote that in the "divine operation" of conversion by the Holy Spirit a believer "experiences new views of divine truth." He or she "discerns in the truth of God a beauty and excellence of which it had no conception until now."[13] At their best, the preachers worked very hard to combine knowledge of the Scriptures with experiential knowledge of the Spirit. "The objective needed to become subjective, the historical contemporary. . . . Scripture without experience is empty, but experience without Scripture is blind."[14]

Just so, Scripture and experience without new, vigorous pursuit of service to one's neighbor is a counterfeit of conversion. At the end of this chapter on "The Kingdom of Christ" Niebuhr recounts, with obvious great admiration, how "faith active in love" ensued from the Awakenings in an outbreak of movements for justice and care for the neglected people of the new society. It was Edwards' principle at work: "To love God is to obey him; the knowing of the good is the doing of the good."[15] And it was Edwards' faith in God the Creator of all things that had impelled him to adopt a sacramental sense of nature and "consent of being to being."

The revivalists did urge new focus on the needs of every human being in particular. Nineteenth-century America abounded with new, organized expressions of concern for needy neighbors, and the religious sources of this concern were overt and many. The "social sources" were less explanatory than the religious: missionary societies for spreading the gospel worldwide; movements for temperance, peace, prison reform, hospitals for the insane, the amelioration of poverty; and, at the center of moral-political controversy of early nineteenth-century America, movements for the abolition of slavery. Sometimes overtly, other times invisibly, this flurry of public activity supported trends to political democracy. In these new numerous voluntary associations, "Christian enlightenment stood behind the rational enlightenment in the battle for democracy, and it furnished ten soldiers to the cause where the latter furnished one, for it dealt with the common men about whom the rationalists wrote books."[16]

Needless to say, it was not a perfect set of achievements, and its Protestant agents were the first to say so. These social impacts of the revivals were as important for the history of the American churches, says HRN, as any statistics of camp-meeting conversions and any psychological analyses of revivalistic hysteria.

These pages are a vigorous example of HRN's theological courage in identifying in the concrete human past the activity of God in and beyond the actions of humans. There this history stands, "a chapter in the past which reaches into the present" for Americans all. It marks our social memory (when we take care to remember), and our "institutions and habits" (whether we are aware of it or not.) In numerous concrete ways it underlay a new consciousness of the United States as a "nation under God." It could even be called a force for our "national conversion" to an awareness that God had particular purposes for this nation, purposes that persisted beyond citizens' refusal to see and to serve those purposes.

If any observer of mid-nineteenth-century America needed reminding that the kingdom of Christ had not yet come on earth, the oncoming Civil War would be that reminder. Momentous political and religious failure to cure the disease of slavery and the idolatries of politics and economics were reasons for new humility among churches and other institutions of a nation soon to be violently fractured by war. God's hope for humanity seems always postponed, so human hope depends on confidence in a kingdom-yet-to-come.

The Coming Kingdom

A religious faith as deeply rooted in a historical past as are Judaism, Islam, and Christianity has to consider how that past impinges on the present and how the present presages a future. The latter will be its eschatology, its vision of the "last things."

In the nineteenth-century American world, a segment of Protestant theologians found the kingdom-come so nearly invisible amid the mixed goods and evils of midcentury America that their attention shifted toward some form of the kingdom-to-come. Twentieth-century Protestantism would distinguish "futurist eschatology" from "realized eschatology" and both from "eschatology-being-realized." Optimists in these debates tended toward the latter, sometimes associated with postmillenialism, the confidence that, now that Christ had come in resurrected power, his rule had begun on earth. Pessimists, premillenarian, begged to differ: great disasters were oncoming in human history, only at the end of which

Christ would come again. By the end of the century, the optimists would supply outstanding leaders of the new Social Gospel, while the pessimists would read the signs of war and rumors of war as portents of great divine judgment in the offing.

Many Protestant leaders focused on the crime of slavery as the object most deserving of that judgment.

> In the minds of the optimists the abolition of slavery was the next step to be taken on the way to the realization of the promise of the kingdom of God on earth. In the minds of revival leaders it was a step of repentance, a preparation for the wrath to come.
>   [Theodore] Weld's vision of the wrath to come was even more vivid than his millennial hope. . . . What can save us as a nation but repentance—immediate, profound, public, proclaimed abroad, wide as our infamy and damning guilt have gone![17]

Weld, a prominent abolitionist, went on to quote Isaiah 58 and its hope for a revival of justice for the poor and his hope that repentance for the injustices of slavery would not come too late for the country to be delivered from dark times already on the horizon. But as he said this in 1835, says HRN,

> It was too late. The repentance of America failed, the method of the Christian revolution was rejected, by the north as by the south. The coming Kingdom was hastened by a millennialism which sang "The Battle Hymn of the Republic," and when the new day came it was no reign of peace and brotherhood: it was called Reconstruction.[18]

With this, the most destructive war ever fought on the American continent, the god Mars took first place to the Christ of the coming kingdom. In the postwar era, justice for the widow, the orphan, and the slave would take on new theological life in the late-century coming of the Social Gospel to the North, but no such gospel penetrated the Mason-Dixon Line; and in the North revivalistic Protestantism retreated from social reform into a quest for the salvation of souls. Even as the great social-economic changes of industrialism scooped up individuals into structures immune to reform by mere individual effort, Protestant preaching sank back into calls for personal conversion to the neglect of collective change. Once a movement of spirit and dedicated community groups, awakenings now took the form of institutions, a drive toward increased church members, and comforts of a heavenly destiny which exerted no redeeming pressure on the earthly missions of converts and churches.

But one segment of fractured Protestantism would embrace the Social Gospel. As it appeared toward the end of the nineteenth century, "it came as the heir of this living movement which had proceeded in dialectical fashion from individual to communal hope."[19] Niebuhr sees the Kingdom theology of Rauschenbusch as critically dependent on the evangelical movement of the previous centuries. Those who, in the next century, were to call themselves evangelicals and fundamentalists—over against liberals, ecumenists and social-gospelers—would sponsor new fractures of the one, holy, catholic church in America. In that situation, the gap between hope for a converted nation and despair for the same, could only grow deeper.

At the end of this chapter Niebuhr is bold to describe the promise of the coming kingdom, as asserted by the spiritual descendants of Jonathan Edwards, as hope for "nation-wide experience" of the risen Christ, of the Holy Spirit at work in the whole of human affairs. In this hope, they were empowered neither by "a rationalism which regarded cross and resurrection, redemption and atonement, as ancient superstitions," nor "by liberalism which denied the divine sovereignty, but by their memory of a loyalty to the kingdom of God which has not been ashamed of the gospel."[20] The evangelical tones of this final Niebuhrian reflection on three centuries of Christian history are remarkable. Some readers of his first two major books may have found such language lacking. Here he repaired confessionally to his own faith. In his next book of 1941 he would specify that confession in yet more detail.

Postscript: Reflections on Evangelical Residues in His Own Time

With that confession HRN could have ended *The Kingdom of God in America*. Insistent as he was on discernment of the presence of God in the human present, he writes a concluding chapter focused on the "institutionalization and secularization of the Kingdom" as he observed it in the fourth decade of his own century. Twenty years before, in 1918, Rauschenbusch had died sunk in despair at the horrors of a World War that challenged his optimism about God's work in the Euro-American world. Now in the 1930s, a new war was brewing in Europe and economic distress afflicted the land that the old Protestant immigrants had seen as flowing with milk and honey.

On the European theological front, Karl Barth's crisis theology seemed fit indeed for a Europe devastated by four years of awful, mechanized war. The world of civilized nations had not been saved from self-destruction by its technical ingenuities, by the wisdom of its politicians, by the discoveries of scientific reason, by the best of secular ideals, or by the highest hopes of theologians. What would save us? Only the in-breaking grace of God, who needed none of these human achievements, could save humans from their idols, sin, and ignorance. Only in the unique power of the word of God incarnate in Jesus and witnessed in the Bible was there any divine fulfillment to be anticipated as one prays, "Thy kingdom come. . . ." HRN later reported that Barth's *Römerbrief* was one of the most important books he had ever read. His underlinings of his German edition testified to how thoroughly he had read it.

Resistance to Barthianism would mark many pages of his own and his brother Reinhold's writings, however. Neither brother liked being grouped with Barth as "neoorthodox," theology returning to Reformation roots. Yet in the vigor of evangelical life and thought in the previous three American centuries, HRN had found much to celebrate and many distinctions to discern between vital and frozen forms of Protestant faith.

In this last chapter he laments the decline of religious vitality as a "movement" into static institutional forms. A movement for him was more like a poem or the themes and variations of a great symphony. An institution by definition suggests fixity, resistance of past patterns to present change, ritual substituted for worship in spirit and in saving truth. Institutions have their valuable purposes; they preserve something precious from the past; but they can obscure rather than open windows to the Living Lord of the world. In denominational tradition, worship becomes a routine, the Bible becomes a "book of statutes rather than an aid to the understanding of God's living will . . . the divine determinism of an Edwards becomes fatalism," the rule of God becomes human law, the kingdom of Christ becomes Sunday morning church, the coming kingdom becomes "a belief in progress." In all, the church becomes "a self-conscious representative of God which instead of pointing men to him points them first of all to itself."[21]

Niebuhr's indictment of denominations as earthen vessels with petrified contents is severe. He writes during years in which some Protestant theologians were working hard for new forms of theologically based ecumenical unity among deeply divided churches. But even more severe is his critique, in final pages, of the theological liberalism against which Karl Barth had revolted. He will not become a Barthian, but he will remain a critic of the easy confidences of secular and religious liberals who celebrate progress without repentance, human ability without human sin, hope in the gifts of human reason as sufficient for facing every human crisis, and images of God that stress "continuity between God and man by adjusting God to man."[22] In such liberalism,

> Neither man with his bigger and better wars, his slums, and mining villages, his massive iniquity, nor God with his wrath interposed any barriers to the constant intercourse of the finite and the infinite, the sinful and the holy.[23]

His ambivalence toward liberal theology will get further expressed in his next book; and in the 1950s he will become ever more the critic of American Christians who believe that the kingdom of God *is* America rather than sometimes more, sometimes less in America.

That Protestants would ever drift into this idolatry will remain a puzzle and a scandal into decades after HRN's death in 1962. In 1937 he knows of fellow American Christians for whom "no greater bliss" seems possible for men than would be "afforded by the extension of American institutions to all the world." He could have predicted that this idolatry would flourish for a long time to come in America, even among those who into 2009 called themselves evangelicals.

Nonetheless, on the last page Niebuhr sees contemporary signs in America of "a spiritual unrest which might become the seed plot of new life" in American churches and in the nation. For faith in the sovereign ruler of the world, can any time lack signs of that rule? For the next twenty-five years he will continue to look for them.

Questions for Reflection

1. The U.S. constitution mandates a division of powers between three branches of the national government. What is the connection between this arrangement and the words that appear on the back of our dollars bills, "In God we trust"?

2. How might Niebuhr critique the statement, "I'm not religious, but I am spiritual"?

3. Someone said in 2008, "The rest of the world is not impressed by the example of our American power, but rather by the power of our example." What in the history of the United States might be examples of what other nations might well copy? In what respects is the American example flawed?

4. When German soldiers went to war in 1914, they had belt buckles with the words, "*Gott mit uns*," "God with us." Others in the war believed that God was with them too. Does God take sides in human wars? What does it mean to believe that God is present in every moment of human history?

CHAPTER THREE

THEOLOGY: "THE NEVER-ENDING PILGRIMS' PROGRESS OF THE REASONING CHRISTIAN HEART"

By revelation in our history . . . we mean that special occasion which provides us with an image by means of which all the occasions of personal and common life become intelligible. What concerns us at this point is not the fact that the revelatory moment shines by its own light and is intelligible in itself but rather that it illumines other events and enables us to understand them. Whatever else revelation means it does mean an event in our history which brings rationality and wholeness into the confused joys and sorrows of personal existence and allows us to discern order in the brawl of communal histories. Such revelation is no substitute for reason; the illumination it supplies does not excuse the mind from labor; but it does give to that mind the impulsion and the first principles it requires if it is to be able to do its proper work. In this sense we may say that the revelatory moment is revelatory because it is rational, because it makes the understanding of order and meaning in personal history possible. Through it a pattern of dramatic unity becomes apparent with the aid of which the heart can understand what has happened, is happening, and will happen to selves in their communities.[1]

Three years before his death in 1962, Niebuhr was one of a cluster of seminary teachers who called their discipline Christian Ethics. Traditionally, in church teaching, ethics was a subsection of Systematic Theology. These

---

This chapter title is taken from *The Meaning of Revelation* (New York: The Macmillan Company, 1961), 137.

teachers sensed that their work had a special academic identity and deserved a special academic society. In 1959 some twenty-five of them gathered for a weekend in Washington, D.C., and decided to organize The American Society of Christian Social Ethics. Forty years later the members of this society numbered over a thousand scholars, many of whom were university as well as seminary teachers. If interviewed, a remarkable number of them could speak of their profound debts to that cluster of professors from 1959. Two had the name Niebuhr.

It will always be difficult to be sure if HRN influenced American theology and church life most in his classroom teaching or most in his books. Behind his written words stood a great mind and a great teacher. His students, who afterwards would commend his books to their own students, had to hope that they could convey to them a theology whose authenticity had in it his and their own personal integrity.

After the deaths of authors, however, books endure as testimonies to what their authors believed important to share with others. Much to the grief of students and colleagues who knew HRN in his classroom lectures, his hope for writing a comprehensive book on Christian ethics, growing out of those lectures, was cut short by his death at 67.

His seven major books will be enough for persons reading this little book to encounter HRN. Which book to pick up first? The choice is not easy. In these pages we have been following his scholarship chronologically, but that is not the only approach to any major thinker's work. For students of church history, *Social Sources* and *The Kingdom of God* can open doors into the complex relation between ideas, individuals, and institutions in human affairs; for a comprehensive survey of varieties of church ethical teachings over the centuries, *Christ and Culture* would be basic; for philosophical ethics, *The Responsible Self*; for the relation of faith to science, *Radical Monotheism*; and for an exposition of Niebuhr's own faith as a Christian, *The Meaning of Revelation*.

That latter book would be the first one that I would most want to put into the hands of anyone really interested in this theologian. Students who define themselves as "liberal" or "evangelical" both have reason to study this book carefully. In his two pre-1941 books HRN distinguished often between superficial and deep religious faith. In *The Meaning of Revelation* (MR) we have a confessional theology of great personal depth and power. No short summary of this book can do it justice. Few other books in twentieth-century Christian theology combine history, logic, prose eloquence, and personal testimony as intimately as does this one. The mind and spirit of HRN are evident in virtually every page.

The Logic of Disclosure

Liberal theology had put much confidence in the human ability to serve the coming kingdom of God in dedicated effort. Barth had proclaimed that human efforts, like human culture, are so many idols alongside the exclusive truth and power of the Gospel. Throughout most of his life HRN was critical of both points of view.

Firm in asserting, with Barth, the critical beginnings of human knowledge of God in God's own initiative, he was equally firm in believing that the self-revelation of God invites us to active faith, repentance, and new obedience in the present moment. The relationship of the human self, responding to the divine initiative, had an analogy, he wrote, to how selves come to know each other in human experience.

> Selves cannot be discovered as America was found by Columbus, by sailing in the direction of a secret and a guess; this new continent must come to us or remain unknown. . . . Knowledge of other selves must be received and responded to. Where there is no response it is evident that there is no knowledge, but our activity is the second and not the first thing. One cannot know a lover by any activity of one's own love nor a hater by any exercise of hate. Loving and hating selves must reveal themselves—penetrate through the mask of eyes and bodies; before the merely inquisitive gaze they retreat into infinite distance. Selves are known in act or not at all.[2]

On this theme, Niebuhr goes on to quote Martin Buber, whose book *I and Thou* influenced him deeply. With Buber, he affirmed that knowledge of an "it" is profoundly different from knowledge of another person as "thou." We live in the presence of an Eternal Thou, and this triangular paradigm is fundamental to the life of faith.[3]

For HRN Christian faith in God begins in the divine self-disclosure, a disclosure that occurred in past history but which, truly apprehended, happens in present moments. Other religious faiths can begin nonhistorically: in philosophic ideas (as in eighteenth-century rationalism), in the suspicion that the empirical world is ultimately an illusion (as in Buddhism), or in a confidence that the human spirit is naturally the locus of whatever we can know of the divine (as in twenty-first-century celebrations of "spirituality"); but every genuine claim of Christians to some knowledge of God "must begin in Christian history and with Christian history because it has no other choice; in this sense it is forced to begin with revelation, meaning by that word simply historic faith,"[4] embodied and conveyed to us under historic names like Abraham and Sarah, Amos and Isaiah, and—most of all—Jesus of Nazareth. In Jesus God was and is present to us in a historical person made vividly contemporary with us in the Spirit who raised him from the dead. We may argue over how to understand this beginning of this faith. We can argue over how best to describe Jesus, his relation to the Creator and the Creator-Spirit; but every honest attempt to speak of the meaning of revelation in Christian theology requires a return to the story of Jesus' life, death, and resurrection. That story is only a beginning, but we cannot begin anywhere else.

Readers of HRN soon discover that he knew the Bible accurately and comprehensively. Biblical allusions and quotations abound. Beyond all the necessary arguments across the centuries as to who Jesus was, what he taught, why he prematurely died, the fact of his presence in human history gives first impetus to the work of the "reasoning Christian heart." Something happened back there significant for all other happenings. In context of this conviction, Niebuhr defines this theology as "objectively relativistic." It is important for the study of all his writings to understand his careful, nuanced use of the terms: objective, subjective, absolute, relative, relativism, relativistic, relation, relationality, and "standpoint." To be objectively relativistic is to proceed "with confidence in the independent reality of what is seen, though recognizing that its assertions about that reality are meaningful only to those who look upon it from the same standpoint."[5] Superficially, this sounds like an overture to postmodernism: everyone who looks on at the mountain ranges of the external world sees something unique. No one view of the mountains encompasses the whole range. No one view comprehends the whole of anything. But anyone who embraces monotheism believes in an ultimate unity of the world. Modern science presupposes the same when it speaks of a "universe." For monotheists God the Creator is the source of such unity. Even when astronomy speaks of the possibility of multiple universes, the monotheist has to credit them all to one Creator. We intuit that there is a view of the whole of which the Creator alone is capable. By contrast humans know only partially what God knows comprehensively. Our viewpoints are always relative to the One whose viewpoint is absolute. Hence the note that HRN struck in his classroom: "We all have a right to views of the Absolute, but none of us has a right to absolute views." God's relation to the world and us is radically different from our relation to God and the world.

Relationality is a concept ubiquitous in Niebuhr's writing on the nature of God, the human, and all true knowledge of oneself and another self. He was much indebted to the ideas and empirical research of social psychologists like George Herbert Mead, who would agree with the famous aphorism of the philosopher Lotze, quoted by Buber, "To exist is to be related." Such a philosophy finds empirically absurd the notion of Descartes that one should begin a human quest for knowledge by spending a day imprisoned in a stove to reach the conclusion, *Cogito ergo sum,* "I think, therefore I am." That beginning of epistemology is undercut by common human sense, which can best be identified as the sense of human communities in which we all grow up and from which we learn alleged differences between truth and error.[6] This way of describing human knowing is best tagged, not *relativism,* but *relationality.* Every bit of knowledge in the human mind comes from internal-external relationships. Relationships are not external but internal to the nature of selves. Compatible with this insistence would be the well-known South African concept of *ubuntu,* "I am because we are," a truth much closer to the experience of growing up human than Descartes' individualism would allow. Our very reasoning powers are nourished by external relationships; and supremely for the life of faith, we know ourselves as persons related to and loved by the One to whom Jesus prayed. Followers of Jesus side with him in his loyalty to and trust in the Father to whom he prayed, "Not mine, but thy will be done." They aspire to join him in his standpoint before the self-revealing One. "Lord, to whom shall we go? You have the words of eternal life; and we have believed, and have come to know, that you are the Holy One of God" (John 6:68-69 RSV).

> In dealing with revelation we refer to something in our history to which we always return as containing our first certainty. It is our *cogito, ergo sum,* though it must be stated in the opposite way as, "I am being thought, therefore I am," or, "I am being believed in, therefore I believe."[7]

This theology, then, is resolutely confessional. It does not arise from any other beginning—philosophical, scientific, or even scriptural—aside from identification with those first disciples in their confession of a new trust in and loyalty to the Creator out of their experience of the life, death, and resurrection of Jesus. When subsequent disciples join in that confession, they too have a story to tell: "what has happened to us, how we came to believe, how we reason about things and what we see from our point of view."[8]

Having taken a stand with that authoritative beginning, however, one comes into a way of thinking and doing that forbids any relapse into the usual human tendency to look for reasons to feel superior to other human beings with their own diverse standpoints—beginnings of knowledge, trust, and loyalty. One is not, for example, permitted by this faith to derive from it a sense of superiority over all other faiths. One cannot judge between basic standpoints; one can only stand in one of them and testify. Indeed, once in this particular standpoint, one has many reasons to doubt that one is superior in any respect to any other human being. Up front in any genuine first response to this revelation is repentance, thorough comprehensive repentance from old mistakes and sins, which plague every human life and plague it perpetually. Permanent revolution begins with this revelation—and permanent growth in understanding of this very beginning. Theology is a process of reasoning from the presupposition of this beginning; and it will always be a theology-on-pilgrimage. It will never pretend to a knowledge of God needing no correction by better knowledge. It might even inhibit theologians from pretending to write "systematic" theology!

So for HRN a Christ-oriented theology is always a confessional theology. As he had often stressed in his two previous books, he ends the first chapter of *MR* with the sober caution that revelation means not only a new closeness of the gracious goodness of God to human selves, but also and simultaneously a new closeness of God the Judge of all the earth.

> The confessional form is made necessary by a revelation which exposes human sin no less than divine goodness. A revelation which leaves man without defense

before God cannot be dealt with except in confessor's terms. Religious response to revelation is made quite as much in a confession of sin as in a confession of faith and a theology which recognizes that it cannot speak about the content of revelation without accepting the standpoint of faith must also understand that it cannot deal with its object [God] save as sinners' rather than saints' theology.[9]

The rest of the *The Meaning of Revelation* is Niebuhr's version of a sinner's theology: relative, provisional, faithful to its beginning; repentant of errors of faith and life in the long history of reasoning by Christian neighbors of the past, but repentant first in a contemporary human neighborhood in which the author is also an unsaintly member.

Niebuhrian Dialectics

We have already observed that HRN frequently employs the term *dialectic* in describing various themes in his exploration of the Christian tradition. He uses the concept flexibly; it should not be confused with paradox, dualism, contradiction, or its use by Hegel and Marx. A better synonym in his thinking might be *tension* between two ideas or observations of the real, two lenses on the world as seen through the eyes of faithful reason and reasoning faith. In other writings he often uses the term *polarity* as synonymous with two-sided tensions. Many of his insights into the nature of Christian faith emerge in prose that reverberates with the rhythms of his careful attention to this two-sidedness.

The tensions run all through the four main chapters of MR. Among them are the following.

Revelation and Reason

To take seriously the pilgrim image of theology is to know how important is the place where one begins but also the clues to the very meaning of that beginning that come as one pursues the journey. Conversion entails future work as well as a right beginning. Experience along the way helps us understand the nature of the journey, where it may be heading, and what its beginning means:

> The reasoning heart must search out memory and bring to light forgotten deeds. But without the revelatory image this work does not seem possible. In the reconstruction of our living past, revelation is the hand-maid of reason; yet the figure is misleading for the partnership is not one of mastery but of indispensable cooperation. Without revelation reason is limited and guided into error; without reason revelation illuminates only itself.[10]

Faith in Our History and History in Our Faith

The object of faith is never history itself. But God's self-revelation comes to us in our history, and the contents of our faith bear the marks of that history. We do not begin with ideas about God-in-general but with the God of Abraham, Isaac, and Jacob, the Father of our Lord Jesus Christ. In this context, no theological claim is an axiom deduced from Kantian reason, either "pure" or "practical." There is no pure rationality, that is, reasoning abstracted from touches of history. And for practice, reasoning Christians begin with biblical stories as interpreted in the experience of the church and other human neighbors past and present.

External History and Internal History

The former is history from the standpoint of an observer uninvolved in the thing observed. The difference can be illustrated, writes HRN, between a beginning to Lincoln's Gettysburg address that might have read: "The country named the United States began eighty-seven years ago." True enough, but not enough true for that 1863 audience assembled on a battlefield: "Four score and seven years ago our fathers brought forth a new nation." The key word is *our*: these facts from our past deeply involve us now. And, as felt by all of us on this battlefield, this "new nation" that those "fathers" founded now has new, portentous meaning for us all. In our experience of this war, we now see that the best reason for our fighting it has been our new conviction that, when those founders said "all men are created equal," they set for us a new repentant task of including black slaves in that equality.

By analogy, HRN writes, we Christians cannot speak of the story of Jesus and his followers without seeing ourselves as continuing participants in their history. When Simon Peter visits a Gentile home for the first time in his life, under the tutelage of the Spirit, he can now confess, "Truly I perceive that God shows no partiality" to one human over another (Acts 10:34 RSV). One has to speculate that now Peter recovered certain memories of Jesus' life and teachings. The "friend of tax collectors and sinners" befriended a Roman centurion too. Even Romans and their tax collectors must be welcomed into the kingdom of God.

Serial Time and Durative Time

In serial time "past events are gone and future happenings are not yet. In internal history, on the other hand, our time is our duration. What is past is not gone; it abides in us as our memory; what is future is not non-existent but present in us as our potentiality. . . . We are not in this time but it is in us."[11] When William Faulkner famously said (in 1950), "The past is not dead and gone, it isn't even past," he was identifying durative time.

Particular Communities En Route to a Universal Community

Human obedience to the will and purposes of God is a long story of fidelity on God's side and a mixture of fidelity and infidelity on the human side. "In Christ God was reconciling the world to himself, not counting their trespasses against them, and entrusting to us the message of reconciliation" (2 Corinthians 5:19 RSV). Niebuhr's inclination was to suspect that God had not entrusted that message exclusively to Christians, but he was sure that Jesus Christ is our clearest lens for glimpsing the universal human community-yet-to-be and, indeed, the human community of the past. "Jesus Christ is not only the Jew who suffered for the sins of Jews and so for our own sins; he is also the member of the Roman world-community through whom the Roman past is made our own. . . . Beyond all that he is the man through whom the whole of human history becomes our history. Now there is nothing that is alien to us. . . . Through Christ we become immigrants into the empire of God."[12]

By analogy to our own American experience of immigration, new arrivals to an adopted country will always be confronted with the challenge of seeing themselves as heirs of a new national history. They may have arrived a hundred years after the Gettysburg Address; but now the Civil War, the Declaration of Independence, and the Constitution, which they swear to uphold, are parts of their history. By arriving later in the history than those slaves of 1619–1865, they get no permission to say, "We had nothing to do with that then, nor did our biological ancestors. So we have nothing to do with it now." Not so: to become U.S. citizens, immigrants have acquired the shadows as well as the bright benefits of American history. They need to remember repentantly how some European immigrants brought with them new accretions to the racism already afflicting the lives of African Americans for four centuries. They have also to remember the injustices heaped on Native Americans who had lived on this continent for thousands of years. As members of a historic political community, we have no right to pick and choose between the things we are proud to inherit from that history versus the things that are shameful. We are heirs to both. It is similar with our religious communities: we have to confess, with Simon Peter, that it takes a long time and much work in us by the Holy Spirit for us to be rid of our racism. The revolutionary pressure of our faith upon our ethical blindness to much in our inherited history is perpetual. Any white American, born in the twentieth century and raised in continuing forms of racism that spill over into the twenty-first, has homework still to do on the bad debts to this history as well as the good.

God's Self-Validation and Our Progressive Validation

Niebuhrian theology took shape as he moved between liberal rationalism and fundamentalist revelationalism. The one, in the name of reason and progress, seemed willing to leave behind as outdated this and that belief of the ancestors (the Scripture, the creeds of the historic churches, various ethical traditions). The other, in the name of the authority of divine revelation, disparaged all accretions to the gospel from human experience, history, and ephemeral cultural ideas. On the one side here was refusal of a confessional stance in theology; on the other, a refusal to acknowledge that human experience, while fallible, is an indispensable partner to our outworking of the meaning of revelation. Every theology, said HRN, has intellectual partnerships, acknowledged or not. For him the partner was historical study. We try to identify the historical elements in our understanding of God's self-revelation; and we do so to test each by the other so that we may understand both the better. In so doing, we may be able to separate the wheat of the enduring revelation from the chaff of once-real but no longer relevant human experience. (That process he will explore in great detail ten years later in *Christ and Culture.*) To claim that one's ideas, including theological ideas, have no trace of ordinary human wisdom infusing the divine, is an illusion that can lead to unconscious new idolatries.

In this attempt to walk between blithe rationalistic religion and rock-hard gospel preaching of the pure word of God, HRN spoke not of "progressive revelation" but of "progressive validation of revelation" by the theological work of scholars and others in academic and church communities.

> Revelation is not progressive in the sense that we can substitute for the revelatory moment of Jesus Christ some other moment in our history. . . . Nevertheless revelation is a moving thing in so far as its meaning is realized only by being brought to bear upon the interpretation and reconstruction of ever new human situations in an enduring movement, a single drama of divine and human action.[13]

The dramatic image is apt. Ideas, memories, images, and personal-social experiences are always interacting in the Niebuhrian mind. Each is likely to have something to say to the others. The first principles of revelatory moments are never immune to being reunderstood.

> We do not easily change first principles but we discover more fully what they mean. By moving back from experience to the categories in our mind we find out more clearly what was in our mind. The reason of the heart engages in a similar dialectic, and it does not really know what is in the revelation, in the illuminating moment, save as it proceeds from it to present experience and back again from experience to revelation. In that process the meaning of the revelation, its richness and power, grow progressively clearer.[14]

Niebuhr then appropriates a mountain-analogy as drawn by William Ernest Hocking:

"A mountain makes no immediate impression of vastness—it conspires with the illusion of distance to conceal its proportions, and we only know them through the journey and the climb." We climb the mountain of revelation that we may gain a view of the shadowed valley in which we dwell and from the valley we look up again to the mountain. Each arduous journey brings new understanding, but also new wonder and surprise.[15]

I have quoted at length from these crucial pages in order to share a sample of Niebuhr's prose, which is so often infused with poetry, passion, and logic—a combination rare in the realm of modern theological literature. *The Meaning of Revelation* is a book so rich in these features, all in a space of less than 200 pages, that interpreters like this author will always be at a loss as to how to do more than hope for a conviction in readers of a short book like this, "I must repair to the original!" Any summary of *The Meaning of Revelation* leaves the summarizer with a sense of having done considerable injustice.

The Deity of God

The final chapter of *MR* is itself a masterly summary of the book. Basic to Niebuhr's Christology is his refusal to make Jesus the one to be worshiped instead of the One whom Jesus worshiped. In *Christ and Culture*, he will argue for a relational Christology: Jesus is God the Father in relation to the human and the human in relation to God the Father. In a searching passage in *MR*, he addresses the question, old in the history of theology, whether any acknowledgment of a special revelation worthy of naming "God" implies a prior knowledge of God aside from acquaintance with Jesus. Is there a pretheological theology? Is God's self-revelation to Israel that pretheology? Or ordinary human experience of awe at the natural world? HRN tends to bypass these questions as temptations to deify some bit of human reason or consciousness which imply the human-centered excesses of liberalism. For him, to acknowledge Jesus as the revelatory moment is to acquire a measure by which to recognize other such moments in the past and the present. Like Jacob at Bethel, we can now exclaim of some past times and places, "Surely the LORD is in this place—and I did not know it!" (Genesis 28:16). Just so, the reasoning, observing eye and the heart of faith bump into the presence of the self-revealing Lord in many a surprising moment and place.

Above all is the contemporary reality of that revelation.

All this, since it is in our history, is part of what we are and does not belong to a serial past. It is our past in our present. From this point forward we must listen for the remembered voice in all the sounds that assail our ears, and look for the remembered activity in all the actions of the world upon us. The God who reveals himself in Jesus Christ is now trusted and known as the contemporary God, revealing himself in every event; but we do not understand how we could trace his working in these happenings if he did not make himself known to us through the memory of Jesus Christ; nor do we know how we should be able to interpret all the words we read as words of God save by the aid of this Rosetta stone.[16]

The final two sections of chapter 4 of MR concern two candidates for the "pretheology," which a confessional theology tends to reject: Do we have a knowledge of the *moral law* prior to our knowledge of God? And are we justified in *valuing ourselves* highly apart from that latter knowledge?

The Transformation of Moral Law

Also old in traditional Christian theology is a tendency to acknowledge that most humans are well aware of moral principles whether or not they see morality as connected to a divine order of the world. In Romans 1, Paul seems to assume this, and both Catholic and Protestant theologies have followed suit. For Kant moral consciousness is the one basic universal in human consciousness, from which belief in God can be derived as an implication. HRN does not deny that men and women possess this or that sense of right and wrong; but he focuses his ethical thinking on ways in which all human moral feelings and all traditions of moral law are subject to great transformation under the impact of the self-revelation of God in Jesus Christ. One transformation is the shift upward, so to speak, from the abstractions of moral principles and laws to the Person, the Self of God behind the abstractions. A Kantian cannot reach a belief in a divine personhood from logical deductions. There is a leap from an abstract sense of duty to the presence of the divine person. The reality of that Person is indigenous to the prayers of one who taught his disciples to pray, "Our Father . . ."

Once the great, sovereign God of the universe invites us into his company as members of a world family, our morals undergo some striking changes. Niebuhr identifies four: (1) a new imperativeness (to disobey a person is more culpable than disobeying a principle); (2) a new extensiveness (everything now is subject to some relation to God the Creator and Judge); (3) new moral self-knowledge (a corrupted self is less able to obey good law than a Kantian likes to claim—"I ought, therefore I can" doesn't deal with our moral weakness); and (4) a new freedom from imperative law into life-in-the-indicative (by grace we have been saved, therefore we are free to love God and God's will without fear of that moral weakness). One might illustrate (1) by remembering Peter's denial of his friend Jesus in a betrayal that left him "weeping bitterly" (Matthew 26:75 BBE); (2) by refusing the notion, popular in twentieth-century economic theory, that an economic system is a world in itself, little subject to moral direction; (3) by the wholehearted but defective support of national wars by religious folk whose "heart" is more enthusiastic than broken at the idea of killing enemies; and (4) by Augustine's motto, "Love God and do what you want," as when wants for peace and justice transcend wants for patriotism and wealth in the minds of citizens.

This last transformation of all our moral laws, biblically based or not, is especially important for HRN. To yearn for deliverance from oppressive law and a transformation that renders us joyfully obedient to the will of God touches on eschatological hope.

> The conversion of the imperative into an indicative and of the law whose content is love into a free love of God and man is the possibility which we see through revelation. Even more than in the case of the other aspects of the reborn law we discern this feature as a potentiality rather than as actuality, as promise of what the law shall be for us when the great travail of historic life is past.[17]

Does the Eternal Eternally Care for Us?

The Meaning of Revelation was completed just as World War II was being launched in Europe by murderous Nazism. Already begun earlier in 1931 with Japan's invasion of Manchuria, the war pressed upon Niebuhr's mind with an intensity of which only his close friends could have been fully aware. We know from an early exchange of views on war with his brother Reinhold, published in *The Christian Century* in the thirties, that he felt compelled to say that Japanese aggression was calling to mind American aggressions. In that memory God called America to repentance. Two years after the publication of *MR*, he interprets war as the crucifixion of the guilty and the innocent, after the pattern of Golgotha.[18] God is present in this war, he insisted, in its demonstration that "retributive justice simply will not work." As of old, the cross of Jesus has transformed old laws of reward for good and retribution for evil. The war is "a great recall from the road to death which we travel together, the just and the unjust, the victors and the vanquished." The only answer to all this agony and sin is a repentance that abandons vengeance and "a reliance on the continued grace of God in the midst of our ungraciousness."[19]

As humans in the 1940s were killing each other by the million, as in the trenches of World War I, the faith of liberal theology that the human soul is of infinite worth was getting stretched to incredibility. So the guns are killing God? In a strange way revelation, as in the death of Jesus, means just that. But to believe that every human is of great value requires more than reverence for the personal self-consciousness so dear to liberals and rationalists. How can we be sure of our value unless we are valuable *to* someone who has the right and the power so to value us? Aside from such a Valuer, in view of the cruelties of humans to each other in history, we have very little unambiguous evidence of the "infinite worth" of any one of us.

In the final pages of *MR* Niebuhr wrestles with this issue, and he will wrestle with it again for twenty years to come. Not often does he invoke faith in the resurrection of Jesus, but here in the antiwar essay of 1942 he invokes it explicitly. In the cross and resurrection of Jesus, God is revealed as one "who is afflicted in all the afflictions of his people" and who has power to grant us "hope along with broken-heartedness in the midst of disaster." Most of all, "to recognize God at work in war is to live and act with faith in resurrection."[20] It is to affirm, with the ancient Christian hymn in Philippians 2:5-11 that God descends with us into our self-chosen hell and that—by a unique exercise of power—God raises us with Jesus from those depths.

A resurrection faith hovers over the final pages of *MR*, but not as in the clarity of the conclusion of the 1942 essay. A claim that the ever-present God and Father of Jesus was present in the gathering horrors of war in the forties could not have been easy for HRN to maintain against the daily war news. We know that in 1944 he checked himself into a mental hospital for two months. It is not appropriate to speculate from afar about the personal, family, and world-social pressures that led to this retreat. But we know from *MR* that the question of the value of human life pressed upon him *vis à vis* the external observation that the universe seems indifferent to whether humans live or die. The crisis in that observation relates deeply to the question of whether in Jesus God is demonstrating how precious is every human life. Up to the point of Jesus' execution, it looks like a very strange demonstration. Liberal theology asserted boldly that human consciousness implies the eternal value of the human self, but how shall we trust that consciousness as indicative of any eternal value of so mortal a self in a world so inattentive to such value in us? What if agnostics and atheists, reading the external evidence, are right when they conclude with Max C. Otto that we should "acknowledge ourselves as adrift in infinite space, the sole custodians of our values"? Viewed from under the crosses on Golgotha,

> The fate of Jesus was like that of all persons we know. He died; and his death, being that of one we value highly, is even more disillusioning than the death of other persons. If the last certainty we have is that Jesus was the greatest of persons, then we may have a certainty beyond this one, that persons do not belong to the real structure of things in this world. . . . We must make our reckoning with a great impersonal cosmos which does not know that we exist and does not care for us, as it did not care for Jesus.[21]

Coupled with his descent into an unjust world and an unjust death, the crucified Jesus reveals God the Father as the Power that transforms human ideas of power as represented in the Pilates of this world. To believe that "God was in Christ," in these Golgotha hours, is to enter into amazement at "what is really strong in this powerful world. The power of God is made manifest in the weakness of Jesus, in the meek and dying life which through death is raised to power. We see the power of God over the strong of earth made evident not in the fact that he slays them, but in his making the spirit of the slain Jesus unconquerable. Death is not the manifestation of power; there is a power behind and in the power of death which is stronger than death."[22]

The earliest disciples testified to that power in their meeting with a risen Jesus. We meet him in the power of the Holy Spirit, who, with Jesus, introduces us daily to God the Father. Such is the meaning of this revelation. We begin our life's journey in this astonishing invitation to companionship with the One who comes to us before we can come to him. As we journey in that faith, our destiny is forever in trustworthy hands.

Questions for Reflection

1. "Everyone has a right to their own beliefs. Truth is relative." This is a common discussion-stopper. How does HRN differ from this view?

2. Given the diversities of beliefs among Christians themselves, what justifies the claim that they are nonetheless members of "one holy Catholic church"?

3. As you think about your own past, can you recall how you came to change your mind about an idea or a point of view in which you once believed? What changed your mind?

4. Non-Christian humanists argue that they are just as moral as—if not more so than—religious people. How might HRN comment on this view? By what standards might nonreligious thinkers determine that an idea once held by them now seems wrong?

5. The Greek word in the New Testament for repentance is *metanoia*, literally, "a change of mind" which is not only intellectual but comprehensive mental, moral, and spiritual change. If all human ideas are subject to change, is there anything in our "minds" which ought not, must not, cannot change? Do religious and nonreligious people have something to teach each other for answering this question?

CHAPTER FOUR

CHRIST AND CULTURE

The kingdom of God is transformed culture, because it is first of all the conversion of the human spirit from faithlessness and self-service to the knowledge and service of God. This kingdom is real, for if God did not rule, nothing would exist; and if He had not heard the prayer for the coming of the kingdom, the world of mankind would long ago have become a den of robbers. Every moment and period is an eschatological present, for in every moment men are dealing with God.[1]

In the acknowledgments page of *Christ and Culture* (CC), HRN allows that one or another of his former students will say of this or that detail in the book, "this is a fact or an interpretation to which I called my teacher's attention." Oh, yes, he writes: we are all indebted to anonymous, unfootnoted "members of that wide community in which all know that none possesses anything that he has not received and that as we have freely received so we may freely give."[2]

Niebuhr's "wide community" of partners in the theological enterprise is wide indeed. He knows himself to be a social self and a history-indebted self. If readers of his three previous books needed any confirmation of that, CC will confirm it in vast detail. Niebuhr says he wrote this book after "many years of study, reflection, and teaching." To write it he must have spent thousands of hours studying documents ancient and recent. His conversation with historical companions is ecumenical. Though dead they yet speak to him. In this he practices what he has previously preached in his imitation of the Roman humanist who said, "Nothing human is alien to me."[3]

In theme and method, *Christ and Culture* again echoes his debt to the German scholar Ernst Troeltsch and his massive survey of twenty centuries of changing relations between the faith of Christians and the circumstances of their surrounding culture. The purpose of CC will be to describe those changes and to distinguish them under a five-fold typology. As indices to the whole of the history of Christian ethical thought, this typology has been useful for many generations of students since 1951. Niebuhr's younger colleague Paul Ramsey said about CC, "This is without any doubt the one outstanding book in the field of basic Christian social ethics."[4] Disagreement with that judgment would be common in post-1951 decades; but like all significant scholarship, it remained as one of those works that had to be taken into account in all future work in the field.

Culture Defined

Niebuhr defines culture over a span of eight pages. His succinct two-sentence definition is sweeping:

> Culture is the "artificial, secondary environment" which man superimposes on the natural. It comprises language, habits, ideas, beliefs, customs, social organizations, inherited artifacts, technical processes, and values. . . . [It is what] the New Testament writers frequently had in mind when they spoke of "the world."[5]

Defined that comprehensively, culture becomes the umbrella term for the whole of human-crafted things, from past to future, in every realm and locus of human existence. It is thereby a cluster of unavoidable conditions for our thinking and doing, including our thinking and doing as religiously committed persons. Niebuhr will demonstrate that no religion, theology, or church practice lacks traces of culture. Divine self-revelation always comes, in human reception of it, clothed in culture. All sides of theological arguments wear some of those clothes. Sorting out distinctions between the treasure of revelation from its earthen vessels is perennial in church history. CC is a masterpiece of such sorting.

A major illustration from early church history is the doctrine of the Trinity. An array of biblical texts stand behind the doctrine; but as concretized by early ecumenical councils, it was imbued with borrowings from classic Greek philosophy. Niebuhr is wary of the orthodox trinitarian tradition while honoring the faith it sought to express. In the introduction of CC he offers a concept of the divinity of Jesus Christ in moral and relational terms. He had long defined personhood in terms of relations to other persons, so here he defines Jesus Christ relationally and morally. What does it mean morally to call Jesus "Son of God"?

> In his moral sonship to God Jesus Christ is not a median figure, half God, half man; he is a single person wholly directed as man toward God and wholly directed in his unity with the Father toward men. He is mediatorial, not median. . . . The power and attraction Jesus Christ exercises over men never comes from him alone, but from him as Son of the Father. He comes from him in his Sonship in a double way, as man living to God and God living with men.[6]

Some modern Christians have found the "substantialist" Nicene definition of Jesus as clumsy and unclear. One may wonder: does Niebuhr's pervasive preference for relationist thinking constitute *his* preferred cultural presupposition? If so, from this beginning he is illustrating in himself the inescapability of some pretheological theology. His critics will not hesitate to point this out.

The Social-Historical Shaping of Christian Thinking about Ethics

Readers of Troeltsch know how relentlessly he tracked the influence of historic societies, with their diverse cultures, on the content of Christian thinking down through the ages. Societies educate human minds. They make it likely that some ideas will occur, and some will never occur to those minds. One powerful example, which HRN will explore in detail, is the gap between an early church, beset with opposition from the Roman Empire, and a church of a thousand years later which conceived of a "Holy Roman Empire" and a collaborative, hierarchical relation between state and church. "That it became possible in theory," said Troeltsch, "can only be explained on the assumption that to some extent it must previously have become possible in fact."[7] Who, in 30 C.E., could even have *imagined* that one day the faith of a tiny band of Jesus-disciples would become the only religion permitted to flourish in all of Europe? The universalistic language of Apostle Paul might indeed have suggested something like it as a vision, but nothing in his writings hints at an all-embracing church-society realm capped by a Christian king and the Pope of Rome.

The dominant pattern of social change for Troeltsch, Weber, and Niebuhr is *interaction* between many elements, one of them being religion. When faithful minds of theologians and practical acts of church leaders respond to the changing conditions of social history, they are not simply in a one-way system of cause-and-effect. Influences go both ways. But the shapes of the normative relationships—the patterns adopted for judging the relative authority of each—are various. Five varieties were discerned in Niebuhr's eyes as he searched twenty centuries of church history.

The Five Types

As suggested already in chapter one, a "type" is a tag assigned to a cluster of complex realities for the sake of distinguishing it from other clusters. Historians are being typological when they write of "the Elizabethan Age," or "the Dark Ages," or "the Age of Enlightenment." Niebuhr's types have to do with ways of thinking: how theologians in the Christian tradition have variously connected their faith to their cultural circumstances, wittingly or not.

A summary of his five types can provide some road signs for traveling through the body of the book.

1. The first type, *Christ against Culture*, is an image easily assumed from much data in the early life of the fledgling Christian movement, but it is not the only type that can be rooted there. Niebuhr names the "Christ against culture" school as radical: "The world" is the enemy of the gospel, a view expressed most clearly in the First Epistle of John: "Do not love the world or the things in the world. If any one loves the world, love for the Father is not in him" (2:15 RSV). Faith in Christ "is the victory which overcomes the world. Hence the loyalty of the believer is directed entirely toward the new order, the new society and its Lord."[8] First John is not so radical in its rejection of culture as was Tertullian, a third-century puritan who made very clear that the enemies of faith in Jesus are often to be found among the highly "civilized" who are "under illusion from their very culture," which must be replaced by real, revealed truth.[9] Away with your Plato and your Stoics! "With our faith we desire no further belief."[10] Then, the most radical of all Christian rejecters of culture was Marcion, who proposed a dualism that assigned most of the world's evils to a creator-god who could not have been the Father of Jesus.

For a modern representative of this type, HRN chooses Leo Tolstoy, who rejected all forms of human government, including the governments of the churches. "The church is an invention of the devil," so also the secular inventions of property, capitalism, science, and most of the arts. Traces of the same radical rejection of culture in the name of Christ occur among Reformation sects, Kierkegaard, and monastics of all ages.

As in most of the ensuing chapters on the other types, HRN ends with a dual appreciation and criticism of "Christ against Culture." The radicals must not be dismissed as simple-minded and impractical. They can be courageous imitators of the life of Jesus. They have often, against their intentions, improved the societies they reject and cooperated with others of unlike mind to effect the improvements. "Given Jesus Christ with his authority, the radical answer is inevitable."

But it is also inadequate. The radicals spurn philosophies which unconsciously shape their thinking; they use the cultures they ostensibly despise; they adopt rules for church government and relation to society as rigid as laws of the state; they compromise with the institutions of marriage and slavery. "The difference between the radicals and the other groups is often only this: that the radicals fail to recognize what they are doing and continue to speak as though they were separated from the world."[11] Then there is an array of theological issues to which they have unsatisfactory answers: Is all human reason fallible? Are Christians immune to the sinful corruptions of culture and human nature itself? Are new laws inside the church really different from old laws in the society or any less likely to become temptations to forget that God saves us by grace, not works? By refusing to see any presence of God in the Creation, how does the radical Christian avoid the Manichaean heresy of a Marcion? Ironically, a retreat from the earthly realm into the realm of the Spirit can obscure the memory of the earthly life of Jesus.

These criticisms lead to the conclusion: "Radical Christianity, important as one movement in the church, cannot itself exist without the counterweight of other types of Christianity."[12]

2. *The Christ of Culture* is one countertype. It is not merely a mirror-opposite. Every one of HRN's types has advocates who are wrestling with a perennial problem. Each is trying to be faithful to the authority of Christ while acknowledging other human loyalties as subordinate but compatible with that authority. Culture-friendly Christians do not necessarily "seek Christian sanction for the whole of prevailing culture, but only for what they regard as real in the actual, they do not reject other-worldliness; but seek to understand the transcendent realm as continuous in time or character with the present life." As William James might classify these Christians, they are the "once-born" and the "healthy-minded."[13] Among the representatives of this group for HRN are certain early Jewish Christians, the Gnostics, Abelard, John Locke, Immanuel Kant, Thomas Jefferson, Albrecht Ritschl, Friedrich Schleiermacher, and various proponents of "Cultural Protestantism." These theologians measure culture by standards derived from teachings of Jesus. They find that the best in culture can be identical with those teachings, that "with the aid of the knowledge of Christ it is possible to discriminate between the spirits of the times and the Spirit which is from God."[14] They seek intelligent knowledge, which infuses their faith with the best science of the day. They are "no more inclined to fantasy than are those folk in our day who find in psychiatry the key to the understanding of Christ."[15] In the fourth century, as Rome befriends Christians instead of persecuting them, these theologians befriend Roman culture in turn. At its best, this type welcomes positive relations between Christians and their educated neighbors and diminishes their temptation to think that all wisdom belongs to the godly. At its worst, in this type, "All conflict between Christ and culture is gone; the tension that exists between church and world is really due . . . to the church's misunderstanding of Christ."[16]

Historically these cultural Christians have extended the intellectual boundaries and membership of the church, served the common good of justice and peace, and called the world's attention to the work of the Holy Spirit among the spirits of the times. But they have not attracted more converts to Christ than their radical counterparts in the church; they have been very selective in their portraits of Jesus from the New Testament; they overvalue the role of reason as "the highway to the knowledge of God"; they tend to ignore the dependence of faith on historical fact; they locate sin in institutions rather than human nature; not relying very deeply on the saving grace of God, they drift toward "self-reliant humanism"; and, finally, they disparage a trinitarian understanding of God by reverting to a spiritualism and individualism that ignore the mystery of the unity of God the Creator, Jesus the Son, and the Spirit. The radical Christian rightly reminds the culture that the Holy Spirit requires rigorous discrimination between itself and other spirits (1 John 4:1). A more subtle account—historically, biblically, and ethically more sensitive—is in order.

The other three types take up that task. Niebuhr associates them with "the churches of the center."[17] Their advocates relate and distinguish, accept and reject, say often "both-and" but always seek to subordinate culture to Christ.

3. *Christ above Culture*, the third type, is best illustrated in the work of medieval theologians who combined appreciation for the works of human construction with greater appreciation of the saving grace of God. They reserve greatest appreciation for the supernatural destiny of the faithful drawn upward by that grace to heaven. Dante is the great poet of this vision, Aquinas the great theologian. The latter's synthetic account of the universal hierarchy of all things climaxed in the heavenly vision of God that could be imaged in the location and structure of the medieval cathedral. In his system, Aquinas

> combined without confusing philosophy and theology, state and church, civic and Christian virtues, natural and divine laws, Christ and culture. Out of these various elements he built a great structure of theoretical and practical wisdom, which like a cathedral was solidly planted among the streets and marketplaces, the houses, palaces, and universities that represent human culture, but which, when one has passed through its doors, presented a strange new world of quiet spaciousness, of sounds and colors, actions and figures, symbolic of a life beyond all secular concerns.[18]

For the synthesist,

> [Culture] is both divine and human in its origin, both holy and sinful . . . a realm of both necessity and freedom, and one to which both reason and revelation apply. As his understanding of the meaning of Christ separates him from the cultural believer, so his appreciation of culture divides him from the radical.[19]

Niebuhr assigns a scattering of thinkers to this type—Justin Martyr, Clement of Alexandria, Joseph Butler, and Leo XIII; but none compares in scope and detail to Thomas Aquinas. Clement lived too early in the Christian era to construct a full integration of Imperial Roman culture with a church still staggering under persecution. But Thomas, living in thirteenth-century Europe, could prescribe "a Christianity that has achieved or accepted full social responsibility for all the great institutions."[20] Thomas can incorporate the "loyal opposition" of the monastics, the virtues of Plato, and the teleological interconnections of the worlds of God, nature, and human being, all in a smooth upward-surging vision of reality that moves from stage to stage and from earth to heaven. The movement is not automatic: "The steep ascent to heaven, though always involving human activity, proceeds only by power sacramentally bestowed from above," via the mediation of the church.[21] Ethics in this system is based both on natural law, accessible to human reason, and revealed law, which partly overlaps with the natural and also transcends it in the superior "counsels" of the contemplative life of monastics whose virtues, however, do not guarantee their ascent to heaven.

In all, it is a synthesis of awesome inclusiveness. It balances reason and revelation, the services of both church and other social institutions to divine purposes. It locates ethical law in the givens of God's creation; it mandates collaboration between believers and nonbelievers.[22] God works through ordinary human work and the extraordinary work of saving grace. All of us, for Thomas, are the "unworthy servants" of Jesus' parable (Luke 17:10 RSV). "Yet these unworthy servants have an invitation to a royal feast" at the end of their earthly days. "All their menial labor is transformed by them by the inner glow of expectancy—not of their pay envelope but of an unpurchaseable and unmeritable joy. There is always . . . 'all this and heaven too.' "[23] As so often, HRN here profiles a point of view, not his own, with such understanding and in such attractive language that some of his readers are likely to exclaim, "Almost you persuade me and yourself to adopt this type!"

But no, as usual, the summary of Thomism ends with reservations. Does it make the Christian too content with the alleged creations of God in human social institutions? Does it lean over too far in striking up partnership with Aristotle? Has it coped with a biblical rather than an Aristotelian view of evil? Has it absolutized the relative by assuming the patterns of the medieval social order? When that order collapses (as it began to do in the century following Aquinas), do the "perennial Gospel" and the church collapse too? Can the dynamic of divine sovereignty in a changing society be reconciled with this static version of the divine order? In a "final analysis" guided by reason and revelation, is that version idolatrous?

4. To many of these questions Martin Luther would answer yes. The fourth type, *Christ and Culture in Paradox,* is a viewpoint that takes with great seriousness the contrasts between God and humans, divine righteousness and human sin, the wrath and the grace of God, God's will and the resistances of our wills, the singular divine initiative that saves and futile human efforts that do not save. This view discerns corruption in all things human before taking care to observe some remnant of goodness in it all. It differs from the radical type, however, because it affirms God's continuing sovereign presence in the world—the contradiction-filled world of sin and redemption, wrath and grace, state and church, hell and heaven. Niebuhr calls this view dualism and paradox.

> The dualist joins the radical Christian in pronouncing the whole world of human culture to be godless and sick unto death. But there is this difference between them: the dualist knows that he belongs to that culture and cannot get out of it, that God indeed sustains him in it and by it; for if God in His grace did not sustain the world in its sin it would not exist for a moment.[24]

HRN draws examples of this type from the Apostle Paul, Marcion, Luther, Kiekegaard, Troeltsch, Reinhold Niebuhr, Emil Brunner, and Karl Barth. To illustrate dualism in eight such disparate thinkers under one type will alert his readers to one of his own cautions: no great thinkers are one-dimensional. Their actual views spill over into other types. Only with a certain distortion can they be crammed into a type. Niebuhr himself is the first to note this and to warn readers against letting the type substitute for immersion in the deep waters of the actual writings of these intellectuals.

Behind the writings, HRN often reminds us, is the experience of the writers in a certain time and place of history. Luther, the most consistent example of this type, lived in turbulent times, and turbulence afflicted his own spiritual history. For him, paradox inhabits the very core of human selfhood: hopeless sin and hopeful divine grace; unrighteous in oneself but righteous "in Christ"; belief joined to doubts; captivity to the Word of God in Scripture while in restless battle with the devil. Similar paradoxes pervade society and its prestigious cultures. Wisdom and stupidity live together behind masks of power. Theologians betray God while occasionally politicians serve God. Cultures high and low fall under the judgment of the Almighty. Face to face with the holy God, distinctions between "the wisdom of the philosopher and the folly of the simpleton" are trivial. Compared to the distance of Betelgeuse from earth, the difference between a skyscraper and a hovel is negligible.[25] Who can bridge the vast distance from God to humans? Only God's very self, and only in the saving, active grace of Jesus Christ, in whom God forgives our sins and exercises unique power to make us children of God.

For Luther, paradox runs through the whole human existence and nowhere more obviously than in the contradiction between the opposing roles of church and state. God rules the world with two hands, right and left. With one he forgives sin, with the other he smites sinners. In sum,

> If the parable to be employed for the previous type [synthesis] is that of the Gothic cathedral, the symbol which indicates the second [dualist] type is that of the pendulum; each movement in the direction of one pole is modified by a pull in the opposite direction lest it proceed too far.[26]

As with the previous three types, HRN sees "virtues and vices" in the dualists. They struggle with experience, not only abstract ideas. They take human sin with utmost seriousness, first of all in themselves. They understand the relation of God and humans as dynamic and changing, as constant interaction between the sovereign freedom of God and the creaturely, flawed freedom of humans. But God frees the faithful Christian to be something of an imitation of Jesus as servant of the neighbor. We too can pick up a towel and wash our neighbor's feet (see John 13:1-5). Furthermore, we can do that in every honest earthly occupation—no more hierarchy in which priests and monks are more holy than ordinary Christians.

But the vices of this type are as real as the virtues: dualists fall easily into antinomianism—"all rules are off." The two kingdoms theory seems to insulate the witness of the church from secular politics as though the rule were "do not meddle." The dualist divide between love as the ethic of the church and the constraints and punishments of justice as the ethic of the state easily results in the paralysis of a social conservatism that shrugs at such evils as slavery, war, and patriarchal families. So we may wonder: Where in the dualist's survey of the corruption that infects the created world is there room for discerning the good that the Creator still preserves in that world, in human gifts, in the prophetic spirit at work in some human projects, and in a providential exercise of sovereignty in other concretions of human history? Is there a split in the very mind of God, between wrath and love? Is there no way, other than paradox, to think about the relation of God's "right hand and left hand"?

5. A fifth type takes seriously these questions. *Christ the Transformer of Culture*, or Christ the converter of culture, introduces the type that appeals most to HRN.[27] He discerns three distinctive theological themes in this type: (1) *Creation*: God is once, now, and forever the sustainer of the world; and what God sustains cannot be totally corrupted by humans. "The Word that became flesh and dwelt among us, the Son who does the work of the Father in the world of creation, has entered into a human culture that has never been without his ordering action."[28] (2) *Sin*: Advocates in some of the other types tend to locate sin in human bodily appetite, in corrupt pagan culture, or in an inheritance of a "total fall" in Adam and Eve. But conversionists see signs of the original divine creation still slumbering, sometimes awake, in a human nature not totally deprived of the divine image. Evil is real, but it has no "ontological" status as in Marcion and the Manichaeans. Humans and their actions display a "perverted good . . . not a badness of being."[29] (3) *History*: for this type it is the time of God's unending action on behalf of human renewal.

> For the exclusive Christian history is the story of a rising church or Christian culture and a dying pagan civilization; for the cultural Christian, it is the story of the spirit's encounter with nature; for the synthesist, it is a period of preparation under law, reason, gospel, and church for an ultimate communion of the soul with God; for the dualist history is a time of struggle between faith and unbelief . . . For the conversionist, history is the story of God's mighty deeds and of man's response to them. . . . Eternity means for him . . . the presence of God in time . . . [and] the divine possibility of a present renewal.[30]

HRN's major candidates for this type are the Gospel of John, Augustine, Calvin, Jonathan Edwards, John Wesley, and the nineteenth-century English Christian Socialist F. D. Maurice. He discerns ambiguous traces of this type in the Apostle Paul and Karl Barth, both of whom seem to escape the net of any single type. In his detailed thirty-page surveys of John, Augustine, and Maurice, he finds all three coalescing around accounts of creation, sin, and history that fit the above summary.

These pages compose tight, eloquent, faithful introductions to the work of all three of these great theologians. HRN's summary of John's Gospel shows how close a student of the Bible he was; his survey of Augustine, how much he appreciated that theologian's response to changing church-state relations without forgetting either the goods or evils of Rome; and his précis of F. D. Maurice, how important that theologian, relatively unknown in the American seminary curriculum, was for HRN's own conversionist theology and ethic. His final quotation from Maurice could have been taken, out of time, from *The Kingdom of God in America*:

> The Kingdom of God begins within, but it is to make itself manifest without. It is to penetrate the feelings, habits, thoughts, words, acts, of him who is the subject of it. At last it is to penetrate our whole social existence.[31]

Maurice has been mediated to most American students of theology through these final pages of this next-to-last chapter of CC. HRN identified deeply with this English theologian and with the conversionist theologies of John and Augustine. Nonetheless, by the end of this chapter of CC, the reader of the book has come to expect a concluding section on the "virtues and vices" of the conversionist type too. Not so: Niebuhr does not pause to invoke a fifth critique. One wonders why not.

Subsequent scholars have wondered too. Teachers of ethics observe that among students who read CC the great majority opt for type number five along with HRN himself. Perhaps, then, a transformationist view bypasses two major problems: Are there elements in the culture of *the church* that do not need transforming (e.g., the ethics of the Sermon on the Mount, Matthew 5–7)? And, in the changing circumstances of history, might not they move a Christian to resort to one of the other options (e.g., was the Nazi ideology transformable)? If all of the types have some validity and all are subject to limitation, why did HRN not grant this possibility at the end of CC?[32]

Instead there follows, for the end of the book, a chapter that his publisher requested he add: "A 'Concluding Unscientific Postscript,'" a title borrowed from Kierkegaard.

The Postscript is a summary of HRN's theological method, the spirit and substance of his work-to-date, and an anticipation of hoped-for work to come. In their rigorous logic, beautiful prose, and struggle of faith, these twenty-five pages are exquisite expressions of the mind and spirit of Richard Niebuhr. Not many duplicates can be found in the realm of recent theological literature. No précis of this conclusion of CC can do it justice.

In the longest footnote in the book, he points the reader to the other modern scholars of the subject of CC, documenting some of their inputs to his own studies of the previous forty years.[33] He then reaffirms the principles that "the types are by no means wholly exclusive of each other" and, more importantly, that no synthesis of types will ever be available to a human mind yearning for a

comprehensive, universal view of these realities. That view can only be the exclusive prerogative of God the Universal Sovereign. For the practice of ethics implicit in Christian faith, however, beyond the study of all human views there
remains the "conclusion" of such study in decisions to *act*: "Each believer reaches
his own 'final' conclusion, in resolutions that involve a leap from the chair in
which he has read about ancient battles into the middle of a present conflict."[34]
    Faith-full decisions, however, have a certain character, derived from the na-
ture of this faith itself.

> They are made . . . on the basis of relative insight and faith, but they are not rel-
> ativistic. . . . They are individual decisions, but not individualistic. They are made
> in freedom, but not in independence; they are made in the moment, but are not
> non-historical.[35]

Especially in the 1960s, there was much discussion among ethicists about the
"context" of ethical decision; and Niebuhr (with Bonhoeffer) was sometimes identified with contextual ethics. Superficial adherents of this concept sometimes
made it synonymous with the view, "Forget the rules, let the context guide you."
Niebuhr could not have disagreed more. The context of Christian decision is rich
and complicated, but in no sense do contexts "decide" an ethical question. Basic
for HRN were the plural contexts of faith, theology, history, and the church past
and present. These surroundings of the "reasoning Christian heart" might be compared to the "fence" that the liberal Jewish Pharisees of Jesus' time proposed to
build around the Mosaic laws. Inside that fence there was liberty to interpret and
argue over the implications of the laws for the contemporary situation of the community. But there was a definable outside—a boundary beyond which no faithful
Jew should trespass. For ethics to avoid both the false freedom of the antinomian
and the false bondage of legalism, there had to be an *ethos*, a structure that was
both limiting and freeing.[36] Our knowledge, historical particularity, values, and
our faith itself are protections against the double illusion of infinite human freedom and the presumption of pretending to read the mind of God.
    Of special importance for Niebuhr was the "fence" that honest observation
should build around "values." His relational value theory, which gets spelled out
in detail in a later essay,[37] has the key assumption: "Everything with which we
deal has many value relations; it has value for ourselves, for other men, for life, for
reason, for the state, and so on. . . . Nothing, not even truth, has value in only one
relation."[38] But to have faith in God who is judge of all things earthly is to know
that truth, right, and wrong are not the same for us as they are for God. To have
confidence in this negative is to be alert to varieties of value-relations in the lives
of other humans and other creatures. The principle has many a practical meaning. Modern understandings of ecology are empirical affirmations of relational
values. For example, trees supply oxygen for organic and other life while the
organic produces carbon dioxide for trees. To limit the value of my wife to her

value for me, is to cut off the possibility of my awareness of her value to other people and (especially) her value to the One who created her. Multiple value-relations sustain real but relative justice. Relative justice becomes relativistic when some relative value is substituted for the truly absolute one, as when a man's worth— or a woman's!—"for his state or his class or his biological race is accepted as his final value."[39]

With like careful analysis, the final pages of CC reassert the social nature of human selfhood. Individual decision-making can never be individualistic. *Contra* Kierkegaard, there is always a "we" present when "I" decide. Jesus was not alone in his life witness and work, nor is he known to us "apart from a company of witnesses."[40] Without companions we too are at the mercy of mere imagination. The whole of CC has paid tribute to the witnesses who surround the reasoning theological mind. That mind is inhabited by a historical past that forbids the decider to suppose that decisions are made "on the spot" of a moment of time. For us, durative internal time is always in each instant, whether we acknowledge it or not. The faithful Christian

> confronts a co-present, a contemporaneous Christ; but this Christ has a history, he is remembered and he is expected. . . . The Christian is a member of a company which has a history of relations to him and to Christ. To be contemporaneous with Christ is to be contemporaneous with one who was present to Augustine as well as to Paul.[41]

As for the polarity of our freedom-in-dependence, "there has always been a choice prior to our own, and we live in dependence on it as we make our lesser choices among the things that are good for life, reason, and society. . . . We choose and are subject to many choices that are not our own."[42]

As identified in this final chapter of CC, the four interpretative principles—the relative, social, interdependent, and historical context of Christian ethics—were fundamental shapers of HRN's classroom teaching in the 1950s, as would be evident in his posthumously published *The Responsible Self.*

In the last several pages of CC, returns to the theme that has preoccupied him for at least twenty years: the nature of faith as personal trust and loyalty. We trust God as the supremely trustworthy Person, and we endeavor to be loyal to God's universal cause. We do so because we are recipients of acts of trust and loyalty toward us among our human companions-in-faith. They are irreplaceable witnesses to the ultimate ground of our common faith—the life, death, and resurrection of Jesus the Christ.[43] That event, however, confronts us with a great "surd," an unresolvable mystery: Trusting in God, loyal to the Father's love for disloyal humans, Jesus perished in a shameful execution. How from that event is faith in the God and Father of Jesus called forth in us? Fact is, it has been called forth in us, and in our experience we have to credit that event as the beginning of our faith in the faithfulness of our Creator. We cannot account for this fact without believing that we too, like those first disciples, have been touched by the resurrecting power of the very Spirit of the One whom Jesus trusted. Now we too "can say 'Our Father' to that which has elected us to live, to die, and to inherit life beyond life."[44]

Now too we can reason from this faith that our record of distrust and disloyalty, our own participation in the fallible "world," is promised a forgiveness and a transformation which forever deliver us from suspicions that our lives count for nothing. They count for much. Of that, Jesus, the Spirit, and the church of the ages have given solid assurance. And on grounds of that assurance we can seek to add our bit to the ongoing history of God's work in the world. We can try to sort out the relations and distinctions between Christ and culture in the confidence that our work and God's greater works are not in vain.

Questions for Reflection

1. We hear sometimes the claim about successful people, "They were self-made." What would be HRN's response to that claim?

2. "We choose and are subject to many choices that are not our own." If so, what then does it mean to be "free"?

3. Consider one or two "hot issues" in American social-political life, for example, abortion, the roles of women in society and church, and property-rights versus environmental conservation. What mixtures of "culture and Christ"—or ideology and theology—can you detect in advocates of various sides of these issues?

4. What do you find attractive in all five of HRN's types? Which one would you most like to *avoid*? Which, to understand better? Which, to see more regularly at work in the life of church congregations?

CHAPTER FIVE

RESPONDING TO THE ONE IN THE MIDST OF MANY

The theoretical work of the intellect needs to be carried out in the context of the Church's whole life; hence those whose special duty it is to do this work must participate in that life if they are to discharge their peculiar duty. . . . The proper work of the intellect lies in the accurate, critical discovery, definition and testing of . . . ideas. But this work of theory cannot stand alone because it is a work of abstraction that proceeds from, and must return to, the concrete reality of life. Moreover, engagement in theological inquiry involves the student in personal hazards because he is tempted to regard the abstract as the real and even to make it the object of his love. This danger can be avoided only if theology is set within the larger personal and social context of a life of love of God and neighbor.[1]

In the fall of 1955, *Life Magazine* published an article on major contemporary American theologians, among whom was H. Richard Niebuhr. Accompanying a sketch of his lifework was a photograph by Alfred Eisenstaedt. Soon after publication over a hundred personal letters poured into HRN's mailbox at Yale Divinity School, most of them exhibiting some version of the inquiry: "When I look at your photograph, I see a face wrinkled with a deep intellect and experience of suffering. I wonder if you would help me in my wrestle with the following problem. . . ."

That fall HRN wrote by hand personal responses to all those letters. Students and colleagues at Yale Divinity School marveled that he would take on such a task. But they promptly recognized that he was practicing a discipline imposed on him by his own theology and sense of vocation.

In the retrospect of this student,[2] all those handwritten letters from strangers and his answers to them suggest several dimensions of their fit with HRN's life and teaching. First was his acknowledgment, as a famous faculty member in an ecumenical school of theology, that Christian theologians must serve the needs of more than students in their classrooms, more even than the members of churches around the world. The "neighbor" is any needy fellow human who, like an injured man left half dead on the road to Jericho, cries out for help. HRN's writings are rife with universals: no thing, no creature is unrelated to the power and care of God. The universal sway of the Creator, however, becomes particular in the realms of history, yielding particular challenges to particular persons and communities of faith. One such particular he must have acknowledged in the feedback that came from this unsought publicity in a national magazine. In this same year, he published the book from which the above quotation is taken, *The Purpose of the Church and Its Ministry.*[3] The book expresses HRN's understanding of the purposes of the church, theological schools, and the vocation of teachers and students in those schools. The purpose of the church, he wrote, is "the increase of the love of God and neighbor" in the world. By that definition, one measure of authentic teaching and study of theology is the requirement that teachers and students serve their neighbors even as they study and teach. The life of the "reasoning heart" requires intellectual abstractions, but to be lured into love for the abstractions, apart from their possible concrete service to fellow humans, is to risk idolatry.

In virtually every Niebuhr book of the 1929–51 era, we meet the observation that we humans are acted upon long before we find ourselves able or compelled to act. No one of us is a self-made person. We are born to parents, located in circumstances we do not choose, inserted into a history of others who act upon us before we are actors. Thus it must have been with that *Life* article and that stuffed mailbox. He had asked for neither. But the letters now asked something from him.

One has to wonder: what did his correspondents see in that Eisenstaedt portrait of HRN that moved them to write him those personal letters? And what in Niebuhr's own life lay behind his sense of obligation to respond to the letters? Naturally we cannot be sure. We do know that personal suffering and the agonies of fellow humans in the war years of the 1940s may have moved him to a two-month withdrawal into a mental hospital. We know also that his wife's and his distress at the illness of their daughter bore heavily on them. And—so some studies of his life testify—in the 1950s he was beginning to wonder if his contributions to the study of Christian ethics were making any impact on the world at large.

Whatever the justification of these speculations, there is much reason to agree with the opinion that in his life as well as in his writings, in himself and with his world neighbors, he walked through many a valley of shadows that challenged his faith with doubt and his hope with despair. What citizen of the twenty-first century, living through many decades of the twentieth, has no empathy for such a challenge?

Radical Monotheism

The sixth of his major books, *Radical Monotheism and Western Culture* (RM), was published two years before his death in 1962. In the late fifties his books and lectures found eager hearing in extra-Yale settings as various as Omaha, San Francisco, Glasgow, Washington, D.C., and New York City. In these years he continued his critical assessments of contemporary neo-orthodox theology, especially in what he saw as the dangers of Christocentric overemphasis on the Second Person to the neglect of the First and the Third. Readers of *The Meaning of Revelation* were puzzled by this turn from his own emphasis on Jesus Christ as the key event in the self-revelation of God the Father; but he was adamant in his worry that for too many Christians the confession "Jesus Christ is Lord" neglects the rest of Paul's formula in Philippians 2:11: "to the glory of God the Father."[4] Trinitarian concepts, in the intentions of Christian theologians ancient and modern, no more violate their conviction of the oneness of God than do the images employed by Jewish and Islamic theologians regarding the same oneness. Moreover, ever and again, in theology and ethics, HRN was wary of the temptations of practical henotheism—the worship of a divinity resident in a segment of reality like one's nation—and polytheism, the relaxed acceptance of any number of divinities who preside over the pluralisms of ordinary human loyalties.

In seventy-five packed pages of RM, HRN contrasts Christian faith, "the practice of trust and loyalty" to the One, with the diversion of human trusts and loyalties to other objects of faith. Authentic faith will transform all the major areas of our lives. All tempt us to yield to the lures of henotheism and polytheism. Henotheism dominates science when its practitioners claim that the only truth about the world comes through scientific methods, a judgment that helps account for the archipelago of the modern university with its islands of specialized knowledge in little or no communication with each other. Polytheism dominates politics when the compromises of justice dissolve into mere catering to unnumbered interest groups. Henotheism creeps into religion when its advocates cease to ask, "How may the one Lord of Creation be at work in other religions too? While trying to be faithful to the One revealed to us, what should we learn from those other faiths?" Polytheism creeps in when advocates of religious freedom justify it in terms of secular peace between rival faiths or simply because all human beings have a right to their own points of view.

Niebuhr's transformationist view of the relation of Christ and culture affects his analysis of the inmost "religious" life of churches, for example, in careful rather than careless praying of the Lord's Prayer, the most frequently repeated liturgy in Christian practice worldwide.

> Radical monotheism does not teach men to pray but how to pray to the One, how so to make supplications and intercessions that they are made in confidence in him and are coherent with his cause. Though the prayers be for food and for forgiveness they are now set in the context of prayer for the doing of his will and the coming of his kingdom; though they are petitions for the self they are offered in the midst of intercession for every being in need of aid and succor. In radical faith men learn to pray in confidence and quietness without frantic efforts to

appease the power whence life and death both issue; they learn to pray to the One who cares for all as though they were but one and for each one as though he were all; they learn to pray as those who expect a change of mind [metanoia] less in the One on whom they call than in themselves. Nothing in man's natural prayer religion is denied by the radical faith; every part of it is reoriented and reorganized.[5]

RM is HRN's most philosophically attuned book. It embodies his turn away from theology proper to concentration on certain philosophical accounts of what it means to confess, "I believe in God the Father Almighty, Creator of heaven and earth." The book concludes with four essays, one of which—"The Center of Value"—has exerted enormous influence on the study of philosophical value-theory in both secular and religious academic circles. Though a summary of this essay is as difficult as a summary of any book by HRN, it is a key exposition of one of his favorite definitions of the aim of ethical analysis: "accuracy in action." In some respects it is a compact mini-introduction to his lectures on Christian ethics in the 1950s.

The Center of Value

In current talk, most of us speak of "values" with considerable inaccuracy. We imagine them (as some imagine God) as oblong blurs that float above the world of human opinion and concrete empirical reality. Not so, said HRN: we are immersed in value-relations in every moment of our lives.

> Value is present wherever being confronts being, wherever there is becoming in the midst of plural, interdependent, and interacting existences. It is not a function of being as such but of being in relation to being. . . . If anything existed simply in itself and by itself, value would not be present. Value is the good-for-ness of being for being in their reciprocity, their animosity, and their mutual aid. Value cannot be defined or intuited in itself for it has no existence in itself; and nothing is valuable in itself, but everything has value, positive or negative, in its relations. Thus value is not a relation but arises in the relations of being to being.[6]

"The Center of Value" brings together his lifelong study of relation and relativism, the relational nature of anything's identity, and the assault on monotheism when any being—for example, human being as such—becomes the one center for which all value-relations are centered. To believe in God as sovereign Creator and Governor of the world is to believe, positively, that God knows the value of all that is, honors all that is, and works providentially to render wrong relations right. "The 'ought' in which the sense of right comes to expression is a statement of what is owed to another being."[7] To say that two beings are rightly related is to observe that the value of each to the other is mutually served; to say that two beings are wrongly or unjustly related, is to observe that one side, if not both, fails to serve the good-for the other. In this analysis, the perennial philosophical argument between the "good" and the "right" as central ideas in ethics gets a new setting: rightness is "the goodness of relatedness in action." The argument has often focused on whether values are "objective" or "subjective." In this Niebuhrian analysis, they are both: objective to one side of the relation, subjective to the other. A tree cannot live without right relations to moisture, soil, and other creatures, including humans. Among the latter, judgments sometimes have to be made between a good-for a tree and a good-for a human who needs lumber. Clashes between value-relations occur all the time in nature and in human affairs, and some of these clashes deserve the name of tragedy. For others, we may have no sure name, as when in the interest of human health we destroy disease-carrying insects. We may do so in ignorance or disparagement of the value of those insects in other relationships—for example, the value of mosquitoes to bats. To very few value-relations does the human mind—from science or ordinary experience—have the right to assign an ultimate judgment. We remain open-minded, if we believe in the Creator, to God's ultimate judgment of the complex world of value-relations. Humility, in the midst of our partial knowledge of the good and the bad, seems mandated for this dimension of real faith in God.

This analysis has acute importance for how humans define "justice" in our relations to each other. Most political conflict, for example, involves lopsided perceptions of, or commitments to, what is good for friends versus what is good for enemies. When Americans go to war to defend their own wealth, power, and territory, we subordinate various interests of the enemy and may even refuse to acknowledge the value of the enemy's life and status as a fellow human being. To acknowledge the value of enemies' lives as equal to the value of the lives of one's own "people" is rare in the history of warfare. That rarity depressed Richard Niebuhr in the years just before and during World War II. Americans old enough to remember those years know how little respected by our public were the lives of Germans and (even less) the lives of Japanese in those years. Persons brave enough to testify to their faith that the lives of all were valuable to God the Creator were often accused of being unpatriotic. The accusation had some accuracy in it: if God the Creator is the center of value, the One to whom all beings are related and rightly valued, then anyone who puts faith in that God cannot put equally strong faith in another center—for example, one's country. To assign only relative value to a country is, at least, to hold that value in a spirit of humility and under a requirement of repentance. In the moment in which this is written, the American public is aware that some 4,200 of our soldiers have died in the Iraq War. How many of us notice the deaths of Iraqis, from all causes, in a number possibly as high as 600,000? Or the suffering of four million Iraqi refugees, displaced by the war?

With this beginning the value theory of monotheistic theology is enabled to proceed to the construction of many relative value systems, each of them tentative,
experimental, and objective, as it considers the interaction of beings on beings,
now from the point of view of man, now from the point of view of society, now
from the point of view of life. But it is restrained from erecting any one of these
into an absolute, or even from ordering it above the others.[8]

Faith leaves to God the ultimate judgment of the values of things that puzzle
and mystify us: diseases, other enemies of our existence, the value of this awe-
somely large universe.

From this essay to the spirit and substance of HRN's capacious accounts of
Christian ethics in his classroom teaching, there were very direct bridges. The
nearest published account of that teaching we have in a posthumous volume put
together by colleagues who mourned his premature death but compensated for it,
as best they could, in *The Responsible Self: An Essay in Christian Moral Philosophy.*
Along with *The Meaning of Revelation* and *Christ and Culture*, it would remain for
many of his students a strong rebuttal of his own doubt that his lifework would
have much enduring impact on generations coming after him.

Questions for Reflection

1. Are you comfortable with the idea that the United States is a nation especially favored by God? Why or why not?

2. From what you know of another religious faith than your own, what do you
think that you and your religious community might learn from it?

3. Considering HRN's concept of value-relations, think of some examples in ordinary experience of "right relations" and "wrong relations."

4. What wisdom is there in the "Center of Value" essay for dealing with political conflict, domestic and global? With personal decisions you have to make?

CHAPTER SIX

SELVES IN RESPONSE TO THE CREATOR, GOVERNOR, AND REDEEMER

Thus Christians understand themselves and their ethos, or somewhat in this fashion. They cannot boast that they have an excellent way of life for they have little to point to when they boast. They only confess—we were blind in our distrust of being, now we begin to see; we were alien and alienated in a strange, empty world, now we begin sometimes to feel at home; we were in love with ourselves and all our little cities, now we are falling in love, we think, with being itself, with the city of God, the universal community of which God is the source and governor. And for all this we are indebted to Jesus Christ, in our history, and in that depth of spirit in which we grope with our theologies and theories of symbols. Could it have happened otherwise; could the same results have been achieved through other means? Are they produced elsewhere through other means? That seems possible; nevertheless, this one is our physician, this one is our reconciler to the Determiner of our Destiny. To whom else shall we go for words of eternal life, to whom else for the franchise in the universal community?[1]

In all his books to 1962, Niebuhr laid theological groundwork for what he hoped to compose as a three-volume survey of Christian ethics. The first volume would have summarized his thinking on the methods and theological presuppositions for a Christian ethic, already implicit in his published writings. The second would have been "The Principles of Christian Action," and only in the third would he treat the concrete areas of human response to the action of God in politics, war and peace, economics, family, and so forth.

Ethics, as Aristotle remarked, is a subject that every human has opinions and knowledge about. That is reason enough why no wise academic ethicist wants to advance the claim that he or she is an unassailable authority on the subject. Niebuhr could have advanced three reasons for refusing such authority: Most of all, God alone is *the* authority for our ethics and everything else. Further, every human and every human community has a unique life situation to reckon with. We presume too much when we pretend to know what decisions others should make in their situations. Finally, in contemporary history the time is long past when an Aristotle or an Aquinas can bravely write ethical rules for governing a whole society with its specialized experts in matters economic, political, and scientific.

Niebuhr's ambition as theological ethicist was quite otherwise. His hope was, not to define concrete specifics for this and that ethical action across the spectrum of human activities, but rather to propose an *ethos*, a context of surrounding assumptions and helps, which might enable the Christian in his or her communities, to make decisions "on the basis of relative insight in the freedom of faith."[2]

The Responsible Self (RS) is our nearest set of clues to how HRN might have written the first volume of his masterwork in Christian ethics. It is almost certain that, were he to read that last sentence, a smile would spread in circles around that much-wrinkled face and he would say, "There are no masterworks! Everything we do is partial and finished only in the providences of God!" One remembers that Dietrich Bonhoeffer said the same in response to his long imprisonment in the summer of 1944: These days, he said, hardly anyone has the chance to produce a masterwork, an encyclopedic summary of a lifetime of scholarship. In the sum total of things, what are we but fragments in the hands of God, like pieces of glass in a cathedral window or a subtheme in a fugue?[3] Dead at any age—Bonhoeffer at thirty-nine or HRN at sixty-seven—none of us is the whole window or the whole music.

One of HRN's favorite hopes for his students was that, in their own scholarship and other work, they would make a "contribution" to the accumulated wisdom of their times. Contributions are possible. "Revolutions" and "decisive breakthroughs" may be ours, but to plan to make them verges on *chutzpah*. At our best, one might say, we are blessed if the light of the divine shines through our small piece of the window without undue refraction. As James Gustafson says in his appreciative, faithful summation of his teacher's work in the posthumous 1963 introduction to *The Responsible Self*,

> Theology, he often said, is reflection on the action and nature of God; ethics is reflection on the response of man to the action and nature of God. . . . If this introductory essay aids the reader in recalling or seeing for the first time how the responsible self is related to the action of God, the Father, the Son, and the Holy Spirit, God the Father of our Lord Jesus Christ, it has achieved its purpose. No one is more aware than its author of its deficiencies, and no one wishes more than he that H. Richard Niebuhr could have written for himself a volume on "The Principles of Christian Action" and a third on "Christian Responsibility in the Common Life."[4]

Of this 2009 introductory essay, let the same be said.

A Definition of Responsibility

In these lectures,[5] HRN says in a prologue that he means to speak as a "Christian moral philosopher," as a Christian who commends to others a certain way of thinking, which they may find valuable, whether or not they can accept the theology behind the philosophy. What is it, he asks, for human beings to be *agents*, to know ourselves as having to make decisions and to act in this or that time and place?

To this great recurring question, Western philosophers have made two perennial, typical answers. One has been tagged *homo faber*: we are makers and doers of things for purposes, for one or another *telos*. Thus according to Aristotle: a purpose defines what a thing essentially is, and in discerning a network of ascending good purposes, we catch an image of the world itself. To be ethical is to observe in action the purposes of being human, the highest of which is the life of reason and contemplation of truth. The classical alternative to this view has always been that of Plato, for whom obedience to *law*, right rational principle, is the essence of ethics. Not purpose, but *duty* (Greek, *deon*, "that which is necessary") is the essence of the moral life, as citizen duty in a rightly structured political state. The ethical human is *homo politicus*.

There are many problems with the preoccupation of philosophers with these two images or metaphors for ethics, but HRN is clear that metaphors for reality are important beginnings of our pursuit of wisdom and integrity as men and women in society. One trouble with both of the above images is their tendency toward rationalism—as though an ethical decision consists almost totally of individual right thinking. In our time, especially, HRN proposes, another metaphor seems to match the actual complexity of our modern situation for discerning good and bad, right and wrong. We are born into a certain history and circumstance. A new history may be in the making, as new forces and events enter our lives unasked-for. Eventually, to these "givens" we have to make *response*, which is different from mere reaction. A complexity of circumstance seems to require that we grapple with a mixture of things right, things good, things unexpected, and things yet to come in our time and place. A better image of ethics for us, therefore, may be *responsibility*.

A focus on responsibility comports very closely with themes in HRN's theology set forth in all his books since 1929: from birth we are subject to the givens of our creation and histories; the influences of our relations to other people and communities; experiences that shape our thinking before we acquire ideas of good and right, and authorities commended to us in our respective historical communities. For example, how shall Christians respond to a terrorist attack like 9/11? Jesus seems to commend pacifism as the ethic for his disciples. How then should Christians have responded to terrorists or the evils of Nazism? Shall we seek to serve justice, peace, and the saving of lives by joining a plot to murder a dictator?

Shall we grudgingly collaborate with a military response to an enemy invasion while still refusing to abandon our pacifist principles and our hopes for politics not based on violence? Can we somehow hold in mind and heart a mixture of hopes and reservations about a war as an expression of our faith in the Lord of history? How, in such a war, is the Lord judging our sins and correcting our faulty mixtures of wisdom and folly?

Furthermore, after a "leap from the chair" into these battles of our time, what will we have learned from that leap for making a better decision next time?

Ethics in this mode is a process that pays due attention to goals, duties, and precedents but is not fixed or paralyzed by that attentiveness. If faith in God means acknowledging the presence of God every moment and place in the world, openness to being guided and taught by that presence is inescapably required of any decision that deserves names like responsible, appropriate, fitting.[6] Such a decision will be the outgrowth of a conversation between persons, communities, and facts in which we finally discern a path of action to which we seem to be called. We are likely to bring to that conversation an interpretation consisting in what we have heard of the word of God and the wisdom of our historical neighbors in our past, though in the current conversation we expect to understand that past anew. This is what it means to be a member of the species, *homo dialogicus.*

In a succinct summary of a very long debate in philosophical ethics, HRN writes:

> Purposiveness seeks to answer the question: "What shall I do?" by raising as prior the question, "What is my goal, ideal, or telos?" Deontology tries to answer the moral query by asking, first of all: "What is the law and what is the first law of my life?" Responsibility, however, proceeds in every moment of decision and choice to inquire: "What is going on?" . . . Teleology is concerned with the highest good to which it subordinates the right; consistent deontology is concerned with the right, no matter what may happen to our goods; but for the ethics of responsibility the *fitting* action, the one that fits into a total interaction as response and anticipation of further response, is alone conducive to the good and alone is right.[7]

For HRN this definition resonated with common human experience whether or not it includes conscious theological elements. And it comports with four theological themes: God takes *initiative* in creating, governing, and redeeming us; we respond to that initiative in *faith* that brings to every situation an interpretation of what may be "going on"; faithfulness requires fidelity, *accountability*, patient waiting for responses to our responses; and finally, waiting in *solidarity* with a community of other agents, without whom we would be bereft of companions in our attempts to discern the presence of God in our multiple, baffling circumstances.

The Journeys of Responsible Selves

HRN's writing on ethics can be tagged "phenomenological analysis" which invites readers implicitly to ask: "Is this how it happens to you when you suspect that you have an 'ethical' decision to make? What makes it ethical? What are you considering as you make it? Have you left out some important considerations? Have you looked long and carefully at what is happening to you and to others? Which others, what past events, what anticipations enter this conversation as you 'make up your mind'?"

By now a reader of these sketches of HRN's eloquent, dense prose will know that his principal interest is to describe and expand the ethos of the human situation so as to open the question of how God is present in the situation. He turns away from the urgencies that often prompt our "demand for ethics,"[8] that is, "Could you please tell us exactly what to do in this situation?" Instead, in *RS*, he surveys these several dimensions and asks: What does responsibility mean in each? What actions of God are already facing me/us? What social conditions must we reckon with? What specifics in our time and history? With what degrees of dependence on the decisions and gifts of others in our communities? With what saving powers of One who promises to be with us always, "even unto the end of the world" (Matthew 28:20 KJV)?

Without seeking to summarize these chapters in *RS*, I will conclude this survey of his lifework with the question: in what ways does HRN discern, in these dimensions, the promises of the transforming presence of our Creator, Governor, and Redeemer? From *Christ and Culture* we know that he urged upon himself and us the hope that our circumstances, our thoughts, our very selves will suffer conversion, repentance, and impacts of the Spirit in the whole span of our daily existence. He describes that whole in four dimensions. For concluding this brief study, I want to suggest how attention to these four might become encounters with a Niebuhrian experience of transformation leading to concrete ethical implications.

In Society

A society, HRN often said, takes shape as a "triad," as a relation between two or more persons who are also related to a third "something." That something may be a common goal as in business contracts, a common cause as in a war, or a common hoped-for future as in a marriage. What if the Third is the One for whose cause Jesus Christ lived and died? What if it is possible to aspire to serve his divine cause? And what is it?

In approaching this inquiry, HRN draws upon a surprising source: the Scottish moral philosopher Adam Smith, who wrote a book about ethics seventeen years before his more famous book, *The Wealth of Nations*. Smith asked: what enables us to make sound ethical judgments? He answered: not by first thinking about right and good principles but by an effort of *empathy*: "by endeavoring to view [my actions] with the eyes of other people, or as other people are likely to view them."[9] One contemporary political leader who read Smith, Edmund Burke, applied this account of conscience to the emerging relations of the British empire to the people of India: how do Parliament's trade policies look to Indian workers? The cause that prompted British business and political leaders was the increase of their own and their nation's wealth. Burke asked them to consider Thomas Jefferson's appeal to "the opinions of mankind" in declaring American independence. It was an appeal to a community-of-moral-responsibility beyond that of the nation. They were identifying a national interest in a cause that transcended the nation:

> Ultimately we arrive in the case of a democracy at a community which refers beyond itself to humanity and which in doing so seems to envisage not only representatives of the human community as such but a universal society and a universal generalized other, Nature, and Nature's God.[10]

As children, Americans learn this language from the Declaration of Independence. In such language we bind ourselves not only to a national neighborhood but also to the neighborhood of humanity, "an ultimate community in which all men are equal and are related to 'the Supreme Judge of the world.' "[11]

> So might people of faith intuit about the actions of the God and Father of Jesus in this history:
>   The responsible self is driven as it were by the movement of the social process to respond and be accountable in nothing less than a universal community. . . . When this monotheistic believer tries to understand his own life, he finds that it is a life lived less under universal law and less in pursuit of a universal goal than a life of responsibility in a universal community.[12]

From this discernment of what God is doing in our midst, one might welcome the coming of a Universal Declaration of Human Rights, and one might learn to grieve for the death of one Iraqi in war on the same day when one grieves for the death of one American.

In Time and History

Philosophic ethicists who focus on law or purpose seem strangely careless of time. For dutiful Kant the great categorical imperative is timeless; for the great teleologues, the future is everything, the past is mere prologue. In fact, it is hard to identify convincingly any "timeless" human idea. Our so-called à priori equipment is a heritage from personal and social pasts. We learn language "with names and explicit or implicit metaphors" for discernment of what our ancestors discerned before we are gifted with new discernments of our own. "The responsive, interpretative self is highly conservative not because it loves the past but because its interpretative equipment binds it to the past." As interpreters we have some past and some future already in mind when we act in the present.[13]

Both as time-bound creatures and as those susceptible to wrong perceptions, we are limited. We forget as well as remember; we celebrate the wonderful deeds of our ancestors; we neglect to remember their sins. We remember our virtuous personal actions; we suppress memory of our faults. Our images of the universal community may or may not include the Neanderthals and the peoples of year 3,000. And, as we get older, we may find ourselves confining our anticipations of the future to the certainty of our coming deaths. To lighten the burdens of guilt buried in our pasts, in view of the certainty of our personal burial, we nourish myths of innocence or offer each other the strange Stoic comfort of the myth of universal death forecast by astronomers. In desperation we wonder: should earth die, can we by our own human effort preserve our species on Mars or on undiscovered moons of Betelgeuse?

Against the power of these myths or images, HRN proposes two faith-full defenses. The power of God visible in the prophets of Israel, in Jesus Christ, and in the present Holy Spirit, is a power to remember our sins past and to suffer the forgiveness of God for the faults in that past. Indeed "the reconstruction of our past can be a large part of our hopes for the future."[14] Many events in our past social-political histories are still "there" for more honest, probing memory of their good and evil. For example, we have much moral work to do in our memories as Americans of our Civil War and its provocation in slavery, not to speak of our Vietnam and our Iraq wars. Christians commit to regular restudy of the biblical origins of our faith. Just so, there are acts-of-God in other times of our past to which we have yet to pay fitting notice.

As for what faith means when we confront the certainty of our own deaths and—more threatening—the mythical image of a universal nothingness-to-come—we simply have to hold and to be held by a revelation of the faithfulness of the One who created us and "a history surrounded by eternal life, as well as by the universal society of being."[15] Is the Lord of Being and History, our Lord, capable of overcoming death with life? An ethic of the faithful "patient" attributes that capacity to a faithful Creator. Into hands more trustworthy than our own, we commit ourselves and every future.

In Absolute Dependence

With Schleirmacher we know that we are not only relatively dependent, in all moments of our lives, on power which we did not originate but absolutely dependent in the fact that we exist at all. So "how is the self to interpret the radical action that flings it into existence and holds it there?"[16]

The issue moves Niebuhr to reflect on the mystery and the imprecision of human trust and mistrust of objects present in our lives from their beginning. The social psychologies of Erik Erikson and George H. Mead illuminate our mixed experience of objects to be trusted or not. Without some experience of trust in parents, family, friends, and strangers we do not mature or continue to live. Infants whose early cries meet no response from caretakers stop crying; they stop growing as persons too.

Were nothing trustworthy in our surroundings, then, it is very unlikely that it would make sense to us to be other than paranoid about everything that happens to us. Shall we find in these "traces" of trustworthiness in our environments a witness to "the structures of faith in the whole realm of being," an invitation to confidence in the Author of all things that are? Some of the evidence is daunting: the cancer virus is fearsomely negative. But somehow even more fearsome is the animosity resident in some of our human neighbors and in our nearest neighbor—ourselves. Does faith's discernment of a universal human community include the murderer, the tyrant, and the drunken driver? What does the creator of those enemies intend us to do about them? Why not kill them all?

To the contrary, a transforming faith in human dependence on the will, power, and love of a Creator invites the confidence that creatures who appear worthless to us are nevertheless of worth to God, the Center of Value. When the surviving concentration camp prisoners were liberated at the end of World War II, they had every human reason to turn on their Nazi captors with knife and gun. That some refrained from doing so implied a conviction, "We must not imitate them." In that refusal was a glimpse of trust in the worth of evildoers in spite of their evil. It was a glimpse of the kingdom of God in an evil time and place.

In Sin and Salvation

In the 1950s some readers of HRN noted that in his focus on monotheism, he seemed to lose interest in the Christology central in *The Meaning of Revelation*. The Robertson lectures, delivered only months before his death, suggest otherwise.

In the fourth lecture he returns to a theme that has haunted his life and thought for many years: how, in Whitehead's well-known image, do we humans move from an experience of "God the void" to "God the enemy" to "God the friend"? The last transition is the most difficult, as the drama of Job classically portrayed. Early in this lecture HRN reviews versions of God's saving act in Jesus associated with the two images of acquittal from our guilt in the universal court of law (Paul) and restoration of the true goal of our being, the vision of God (Aquinas). Neither of these versions offers a salvation that matches Job's and H. Richard Niebuhr's deepest felt need: redemption from our distrust of the One who made us, governs us, judges us, and confronts us in confusing arrays of good and evil, right and wrong, in our past and in our present. Like Paul Tillich, HRN found the heart of his religious perplexity less in anxiety about sin and death than in anxiety about the meaning of an existence in which power lacks goodness and goodness lacks power. Is this One, present in all being, really our enemy, not our friend? Sinful we are, but can we nonetheless believe that God is "love worthy and loving"?[17]

Job's cry "Though he slay me, yet will I trust in him" would be one answer, but it fits neither contemporary translations of Job 13:15 (KJV)[18] nor HRN's theology. Salvation in that theology would be "liberty to interpret in trust all that happens to us."[19] Niebuhrian faith finds that liberty in the man Jesus, crucified to death and risen from death. Close to paradox as it is, the death of Jesus and supremely the resurrection remain for him the window through which we glimpse the trustworthiness of God and the door opened to us to "a universal teleology of resurrection rather than a universal teleology of entombment." The answer to our greatest anxieties, we confess, is in

> the response of trust by a man who was sent into life and sent into death and to whom answer was made in his resurrection from the dead. Of that resurrection we may know no more than that he lives and is powerful over us and among us. . . . However we fit it into the various schemes of rational understanding of this our life, we must always say about the event: "It reconciled and it reconciles us to God." [Through this event,] we have been led and are being led to *metanoia*, to the reinterpretation of all our interpretations of life and death.[20]

That the life of this great theologian was cut short before he could explore with us many another "reinterpretation," the ecumenical Christian world will long regret. In these, some of the last pages which he wrote, however, there appears the conclusion that remains the heart of his own faith, hope, and love: the world we inhabit is inhabited too by "the Spirit who raised Jesus from the dead." Niebuhr's confessional theology and his ethics of response-ability takes heart from the faith of Romans 8. Not only as a testified-to event but as a living presence, the resurrection of Jesus makes all the difference in ushering us from distrust to trust in the God and Father of that one, crucified and risen. It has made a difference in the world at large, whether or not the world of nonbelievers and different-believers join in the confessions of Romans 8. What some of us have to say is, "In our biographies as in our human history the process of reconciliation has begun; at no point is it complete."[21] The creative, governing, and redeeming work of the Spirit goes on—in our pasts, in us the living, in lives still to come.

With that confession, the lifework of H. Richard Niebuhr ended. That we should still be reading his words is a tribute not only to him but also to the abiding power of that Spirit.

Questions for Reflection

1. As you think about your whole life to date, where in it might you identify the power and presence of your Creator?

2. HRN perceived that, whether or not one believes that Jesus rose from the dead, faith in that event has made a tangible, practical impact on the history of the past two thousand years. Can you identify any such impacts?

3. We have seen in recent years politicians, terrorists, and religious leaders appeal to "the will of God" for this and that action. Are such claims credible? Dangerous? Or believable only by certain standards and tests? What standards and tests are central for the theology of H. Richard Niebuhr?

NOTES

Introduction

1. The text of this sermon, undated, appears in a collection of previously unpublished writings, in *H. Richard Niebuhr: Theology, History, and Culture*, ed. William Stacy Johnson, foreword Richard R. Niebuhr (New Haven: Yale University Press, 1989), 208–14. Professor Johnson's Introduction to the collection is an excellent summary of both HRN's biography and the themes of his theology. I am much indebted to him, here and in other places below.

2. HRN, "Theology in the University," in *Radical Monotheism and Western Culture* (New York: Harper and Brothers, 1960), 98–99.

3. Second-most numerous, if one counts all immigrants from all of the British Isles including Ireland.

4. Johnson, Introduction, xxxiii.

5. Cf. *The Meaning of Revelation* (New York: Macmillan, 1941), 185–86, and Johnson, Introduction, xviii.

1. Faith and Idolatry in Church History

1. *The Social Sources of Denominationalism* (SS) (New York: Meridian Books, 1957), 274–75.

2. "The Nature and Existence of God," essay published in 1943 in *Motive* and reprinted as "Faith in Gods and in God," in *Radical Monotheism and Western Culture* (New York: Harper and Brothers, 1960), 119.

3. Ibid., 125–26. Note here the kinship with the theology of Karl Barth. We do not reason or experience our way to belief in God. God makes His or Her way to us.

4. Niebuhr and all the theologians he quotes lived before feminist scholars called attention to the ways in which gendered language can be implicitly sexist. Had he lived into the 1970s, it is likely that he would have seen the justice of a turn toward gender-neutral language in our time. Outside of quotations, this book observes the gender-neutral rule. But the awkwardness of editing historical texts of our predecessors to fit this justified new awareness does not, in my opinion, seem justified.

5. SS, 133.

6. SS, 32.

7. SS, 28.

8. SS, 42.

9. SS, 39.

10. SS, 72. But he wrote this without anticipating the rise of Pentecostal churches in the twentieth century, especially in Africa and Latin America.

11. SS, 82–86.

12. SS, 87.

13. SS, 101. HRN draws generously here from R. H. Tawney's *Religion and the Rise of Capitalism*, in which Tawney criticizes the familiar thesis that Calvinism empowered that rise in a one-directional influence. In a footnote, HRN writes: "The theory adopted in this chapter is that we are dealing with interacting phases of a culture rather than with a relation of cause and effect, operating in one direction only." This approach inclines Niebuhr, throughout his studies of religion in history, to look for the changing degrees of mutuality between social and religious variables, especially in the transitions from one generation to the next. Cf. SS, footnote 9, 288.

14. SS, 99.

15. SS, 107–8.

16. SS, 131. For example, the superscription of the 1647 Westminster Confession contains the words, "Now by Authority of Parliament Sitting at Westminster."

17. SS, 140.

18. SS, 153.

19. SS, 167.

20. SS, 160.

21. SS, 184.

22. SS, 185.

23. SS, 195.

24. SS, 223.

25. SS, 238. There are reasons to object to this claim if "modern times" are not to comprise a time at least as early as the sixteenth century when the Catholic missionary to the Aztecs, Bartolomé de Las Casas, objected to the enslavement of Indians in a letter to the Pope, who replied that instead it would be all right to enslave Africans. Historians of racism might also object that white-vs-black prejudice is old in Western culture, e.g., in the writings of Aristotle. But HRN wants to be sure in this chapter that American Christians will understand how deeply and uniquely their species of racism was influenced by the presence of African slaves in the political and economic center of the New World and its democracy.

26. SS, 263.

27. SS, 274.

28. SS, 283.

29. Gary Dorrien, *The Making of American Liberal Theology: Idealism, Realism, and Modernity, 1900–1950* (Louisville: Westminster John Knox, 2003), 556.

30. SS, 277–78.

31. SS, 284.

32. SS, 277.

2. The Kingdom of God in America

1. *The Kingdom of God in America* (KG) (New York: Harper and Brothers, 1959), 13.

2. *KG*, viii.

3. *KG*, x.

4. *KG*, x.

5. *KG*, 30.

6. "Protestantism was never liberal in the sense that it made the free man the starting point of its theology or its ethics. The human freedom of which it spoke was not a presupposition but a goal; so far as man was concerned it presupposed his bondage to sin. Its real starting point was the free God." There follows the famous quotation from John Calvin: "We are not our own. . . . We are God's; therefore let his wisdom and will preside in all our actions." *KG*, 24–25.

7. *KG*, 43.

8. *KG*, 49.

9. This was Quaker leader Rufus Jones's image, and HRN notes that "the 'curious zigzag' is descriptive of the whole course of American Protestantism." *KG*, 64.

10. *KG*, 64.

11. *KG*, 92, 95.

12. *KG* , 105. When he writes this, HRN sounds akin to his brother Reinhold's suspicion of the machinations of the human ego.

13. *KG*, Archibald Alexander, quoted 106–7.

14. *KG*, 109.

15. *KG*, 112–13. In this passage HRN puts his phrase from *Social Sources*—"the fellowship of love"—in a more comprehensive theological context than he did in that former book. "Love of neighbor" is in no simple sense the essence of Christianity. Other elements have to be present in the definition of this love: divine sovereignty, divine grace that delivers natural human love from its partiality, and love due to God as prerequisite for human ability to show due love to neighbors.

16. *KG*, 124.

17. *KG*, 159.

18. *KG*, 160.

19. *KG*, 161.

20. *KG*, 163.

21. *KG*, 173, 176, 179.

22. *KG*, 192.

23. *KG*, 192.

3. Theology: "The Never-ending Pilgrims' Progress"

1. *MR*, 109.

2. *MR*, 145–46.

3. Years later in 1958, HRN paid moving tribute to Buber on the latter's eightieth birthday. "When I have read what he has written it was something like a letter addressed to me." In this tribute he reflects on the absence of the self in most write-ups of scientific discoveries. Science tells us about the world objectively, but it seldom shares knowledge of the

scientist. It is a much neglected truth. "This is the situation in which Professor Buber has worked among us as witness to the truth, namely to truth in the inward parts, between companion selves, trueness to man before the trueness of God. . . . The Eternal 'Thou'— alien and stranger to us more than self and truth; present always, always ignored, always passed by; the Affirmer who is denied, and affirmed in denial." "Address on Martin Buber's Eightieth Birthday," in *H. Richard Niebuhr: Theology, History, and Culture*, ed. William Stacy Johnson, foreword Richard R. Niebuhr (New Haven: Yale University Press, 1996), 137–39.

4. MR, 22.

5. MR, 22.

6. MR, 15.

7. MR, 140.

8. MR, 41.

9. MR, 42.

10. MR, 121. These sentences express something of HRN's critique of Karl Barth.

11. MR, 69.

12. MR, 115–16.

13. MR, 135–36.

14. MR, 135–36.

15. MR, 136–37.

16. MR, 154.

17. MR, 170–71. As HRN wrote this, a German Christian, Dietrich Bonhoeffer, would write in his *Ethics* that the indicative of God's living presence to us in the mixed good and evil of one's times permits us in freedom to take an untraditional, risky view of the moral law by giving final authority to the living will of God in our own times. "Thou shalt not murder" was for Bonhoeffer in the 1930s an invitation to become a pacifist. But as the evil of Nazism came to a climax in World War II, he came to believe that Hitler's death would save many lives. So he joined the plotters of the July 20, 1944, attempt to assassinate this head of state. At the end of his *Institutes*, John Calvin reasoned in similar fashion that tyrants, as an extreme measure, could be assassinated. But neither theologian was willing to make a law, "Thou shalt assassinate evil leaders." The living will of God, active in contemporary moments, still has the last word.

18. Cf. "The Grace of Doing Nothing," *The Christian Century* 49 (March 23, 1932), 378–80. Cf. Niebuhr's subsequent essays, "War as the Judgment of God" and "War as Crucifixion" (May 13, 1942, and April 28, 1943), also in the *Century*, as republished with essays by James T. Johnson, Alan Geyer, and John H. Yoder from the 1990s in *War as Crucifixion: Essays on Peace, Violence, and "Just War"* (Chicago: The Christian Century, 2002).

19. In *War as Crucifixion*, 27–29.

20. "War as the Judgment of God," in *War as Crucifixion*, 23.

21. MR, 149–50.

22. MR, 187.

4. Christ and Culture

1. *Christ and Culture* (CC) (New York: Harper and Brothers, 1951), 228–29.

2. CC, ix.

3. *MR*, 115–16. Cf. Hebrews 11:4.

4. From the cover of the paperback edition, 1956. Ramsey was one of the founders of the American Society of Christian Ethics, a longtime teacher at Princeton, and editor of the Complete Works of Jonathan Edwards subsequent to Niebuhr's death.

5. CC, 32.

6. CC, 29.

7. Ernst Troeltsch, *The Social Teaching of the Christian Churches*, vol. 1, trans. Olive Wyon (New York: Macmillan, 1931), 236.

8. CC, 48.

9. CC, 53.

10. CC, 54.

11. CC, 75–76.

12. CC, 82.

13. CC, 83–84.

14. CC, 108.

15. CC, 86.

16. CC, 90–91.

17. CC, 116.

18. CC, 130.

19. CC, 121.

20. CC, 128.

21. CC, 133.

22. In a twenty-first-century world of the West that is newly aware of Islam, it is worth noting that Thomas wrote at a time when European theologians and philosophers were discovering the great Islamic scholars. Dialogue with them is frequent in Thomas' *Summa Theologica*.

23. CC, 144.

24. CC, 156.

25. CC, 152–53. Betelgeuse, a star in our galaxy, is eight light-years distant from earth.

26. From HRN's 1942 outline for CC, page 15 in Glen H. Stassen, D. M. Yeager, and John Howard Yoder, *Authentic Transformation: A New Vision of Christ and Culture* (Nashville: Abingdon, 1996).

27. One of the issues that critics will debate is whether or not HRN made good on his claim that typological descriptions need not imply an argument for the superiority of one type over another. See page 47 in this volume for his obvious personal preference for the fifth type.

28. CC, 193.

29. CC, 194.

30. CC, 194–95.

31. CC, 228, a quotation from F. D. Maurice, *The Lord's Prayer* (Cambridge: Macmillan, 1861), 38. There follows from page 228 the quotation that heads this chapter of this book, above.

32. This argument is spelled out in rich detail in the recent volume, *Authentic Transformation: A New Vision of Christ and Culture*, by Glen H. Stassen, D.M. Yeager, and the late John Howard Yoder (Nashville: Abingdon, 1996). Yoder makes a strong case for the enduring authority of key ethical teachings of Jesus in the culture of the church, and he criticizes CC for (1) neglecting concrete principles for ethical guidance in this and other writings, (2) underestimating the forming ethical influence of the church as a congregational community, and (3) so describing all five types as to lead, from the beginning, to a

preference for type five. Stassen and Yeager see the pertinence of these criticisms; but, drawing on the whole of HRN's work (as Yoder does not), they see in HRN more concretion of ethical principles than does Yoder, and they believe that HRN's books should be read as invitations to individuals, churches, and other communities to read all the signs of divine activity in their own times and places. That activity has included and still does include (what the author of the NT Book of Acts phrased as) "all that Jesus began to do and teach" (Acts 1:1 RSV).

33. His list includes the following: Baillie, Barth, Berdyaev, Brunner, Cochrane, Dawson, Eliot, Maritain, Reinhold Niebuhr, Reckitt, Tillich, Toynbee, Leo XIII, and current papers from the ecumenical conferences of the 1930s and 1940s.

34. CC, 233.

35. CC, 233.

36. So described by Lehmann in lectures at Harvard Divinity School, Spring 1960. The Greek word *ethos* can be translated "a fence for confining and safekeeping of farm animals." Cf. Paul Lehmann, *Ethics in a Christian Context* (New York: Harper and Brothers, 1963).

37. "The Center of Value," written simultaneously with CC and published in *Moral Principles of Action*, ed. Ruth Nanda Ashen (New York: Harper and Row, 1952) and later in HRN's own *Radical Monotheism*, 100–13.

38. CC, 237.

39. CC, 240.

40. CC, 245.

41. CC, 258.

42. CC, 250–51.

43. In this definition, HRN notes, he has been influenced by Josiah Royce's *Philosophy of Loyalty* and *The Problem of Christianity*.

44. CC, 255.

5. Responding to the One in the Midst of Many

1. *The Purpose of the Church and Its Ministry: Reflections on the Aims of Theological Education*, in collaboration with Daniel Day Williams and James M. Gustafson (New York: Harper and Brothers, 1956), 128–29.

2. I enrolled in Yale Divinity School in this fall of 1955 and did three quarters of work in his classes through the spring of 1956. Two of those quarters were in his survey course on Christian Ethics.

3. The book is his major contribution to the final report of the "Survey of Theological Education in the United States and Canada," conducted by the Association of Theological Schools. His chief collaborators in this volume were Daniel Day Williams of Union Theological Seminary in New York and his student, new faculty colleague, James M. Gustafson.

4. Cf. *Radical Monotheism and Western Culture* (RM) (New York: Harper and Brothers, 1960), 59.

5. RM, 54.

6. RM, 107.

7. RM, 108–9.

8. RM, 112.

6. Selves in Response to the Creator, Governor, and Redeemer

1. *The Responsible Self: An Essay in Christian Moral Philosophy* (*RS*), foreword Richard R. Niebuhr and introduction James M. Gustafson (New York: Harper and Row, 1978), 178. This is the concluding paragraph of the book and the essay entitled, "Responsibility and Christ." James Gustafson says of this and the accompanying essay, "Metaphors and Morals," that we read here examples of how Niebuhr, "the philosopher of the Christian life," explored a God-centered life of responsibility in his class lectures (p. 40).

2. Cf. *CC*, 234.

3. Cf. Dietrich Bonhoeffer, *Letters and Papers from Prison*, enlarged edition, ed. Eberhard Bethge (New York: Macmillan, 1971), 219.

4. *RS*, 40–41.

5. The six main chapters of *RS* were delivered in 1960–62 as lectures, in whole or part, as the Robertson Lectures at Glasgow University, as the Earl Lectures at the Pacific School of Religion, and as addresses at the Riverside Church in New York. The latter was cut short by Niebuhr's illness in early 1962.

6. The Greek *cathekontic*, or fittingness, he suggested as a technical word for this image. *RS*, 87.

7. *RS*, 60–61.

8. Emil Brunner's book of 1930, *The Divine Imperative*, used this phrase to describe the mood of the period.

9. Adam Smith, *The Theory of Moral Sentiments*, quoted in *RS*, note 8, 75. Most economists and business leaders, prone to quote Smith's later *The Wealth of Nations*, are little aware of his earlier book, in which he considerably qualifies economic individualism with this account of the social nature of the development of personal conscience.

10. *RS*, 86.

11. *RS*, 86.

12. *RS*, 85, 88–89.

13. *RS*, 96–97.

14. *RS*, 102.

15. *RS*, 107.

16. *RS*, 115.

17. *RS*, 142.

18. Alternate translations vary greatly. (1) NEB: "If he would slay me, I should not hesitate [to argue my case before him]." (2) NRSV: "See, he will kill me; I have no hope; but I will defend my ways to his face." (3) New Jerome Biblical Commentary, page 475: "He may (or will) slay me—I hope for nothing else—yet I will defend. . . ."

19. *RS*, 142.

20. *RS*, 143.

21. *RS*, 144.

SELECTED BIBLIOGRAPHY

Books Published in HRN's Lifetime

Original Date		Abbreviation
1929	*The Social Sources of Denominationalism.* Living Age Books; New York: Meridian Books, 1957.	SS
1937	*The Kingdom of God in America.* Harper Torchbooks; New York: Harper and Brothers, 1959.	KG
1941	*The Meaning of Revelation.* Macmillan Paperbacks; New York: Macmillan, 1961.	MR
1951	*Christ and Culture.* Harper Torchbooks; New York: Harper and Brothers, 1956.	CC
1955	*Christian Ethics: Sources of the Living Tradition.* Edited with Waldo Beach. New York: The Ronald Press Company, 1955.	
1956	*The Purpose of the Church and Its Ministry.* In collaboration with Daniel Day Williams and James M. Gustafson. New York: Harper and Brothers, 1956.	PC
1960	*Radical Monotheism and Western Culture.* New York: Harper and Brothers, 1960.	RM

Books Published Posthumously

1963	*The Responsible Self: An Essay in Christian Moral Philosophy.* Foreword by Richard R. Niebuhr and introduction by James M. Gustafson. Harper Paperback; New York: Harper & Row, 1978.	RS

| 1989 | Faith on Earth: An Inquiry into the Structure of Human Faith. Edited by Richard R. Niebuhr. New Haven: Yale University Press, 1989. | FE |

1996   *H. Richard Niebuhr: Theology, History, and Culture: Major Unpublished Writings.* Edited by William Stacy Johnson, foreword by Richard R. Niebuhr. New Haven: Yale University Press, 1996.

Selected Articles and Essays

1931   "The Social Gospel and the Liberal Theology." *The Keryx* 22/8:13.

1932–43   Reinhold Niebuhr, James Turner Johnson, Alan Geyer, John Howard Yoder, and H. R. Niebuhr. *War as Crucifixion: Essays on Peace, Violence, and "Just War."* Chicago: The Christian Century Press, 2002.

     "The Grace of Doing Nothing," 5–9.
     "The Only Way into the Kingdom of God," 15–16.
     "War as the Judgment of God," 17–23.
     "War as Crucifixion," 24–29.

1932   "Faith, Works, and Social Salvation." *Religion in Life* 1:426–30.

1936   "The Attack on the Social Gospel." *Religion in Life* 5:176.

1939   "The Christian Evangel and Social Culture." *Religion in Life* 8/1:44–48.

1946   "The Responsibility of the Church for Society" in *The Gospel, the Church, and the World.* Edited by Kenneth Scott Latourette. Interseminary Series, Book 3. New York: Harper and Brothers (1946): 111–33.

1948   "The Gift of Catholic Vision." *Theology Today*, 4:507–21.

1988   "The Social Gospel and the Mind of Jesus," *Journal of Religious Ethics* 16/1:115–27.

Secondary Studies

(*) Major Recommendations

Diefenthaler, Jon, *H. Richard Niebuhr: A Lifetime of Reflection on the Church and the World.* Macon: Mercer University Press, 1986.

Fowler, James W. *To See the Kingdom: The Theological Vision of H. Richard Niebuhr.* Nashville: Abingdon, 1974.

Godsey, John D. *The Promise of H. Richard Niebuhr.* Philadelphia: Lippincott, 1970.

Grant, C. David, *The Center of Value: Value Theory in the Theology of H. Richard Niebuhr.* Fort Worth: Texas Christian University Press, 1984.

Irish, Jerry A., *The Religious Thought of H. Richard Niebuhr.* Atlanta: John Knox, 1983.

Kliever, Lonnie. *H. Richard Niebuhr.* Waco: Word, 1977.

Ottati, Douglas P. *Meaning and Method in H. Richard Niebuhr's Theology.* Washington: University Press of America, 1982.

(*)Ramsey, Paul (ed.). *Faith and Ethics: The Theology of H. Richard Niebuhr.* New York: Harper and Brothers, 1957.

Scriven, Charles. *The Transformation of Culture: Christian Social Ethics After H. Richard Niebuhr.* Scottdale, Penn.: Herald Press, 1988.

Stassen, Glen. *The Sovereignty of God in the Theological Ethics of H. Richard Niebuhr.* PhD dissertation, Duke University, 1967.

(*)Stassen, Glen, D. M. Yeager, and John Howard Yoder. *Authentic Transformation: A New Vision of Christ and Culture.* Nashville: Abingdon, 1996.

INDEX